The Science of Narcissism

CRAFTED BY SKRIUWER

Copyright © 2024 by Skriuwer.

All rights reserved. No part of this book may be used or reproduced in any form whatsoever without written permission except in the case of brief quotations in critical articles or reviews.

For more information, contact : **kontakt@skriuwer.com** (www.skriuwer.com)

TABLE OF CONTENTS

CHAPTER 1: INTRODUCTION TO NARCISSISM

- *Exploration of the term "narcissism" and its background*
- *Difference between normal confidence and harmful self-focus*
- *Initial clues about how these traits can shape behavior*

CHAPTER 2: EARLY SIGNS OF NARCISSISTIC BEHAVIOR

- *Patterns in young children that hint at self-obsessed tendencies*
- *Why certain early habits may lead to stronger narcissistic traits later*
- *Role of parents and caregivers in guiding or reinforcing behaviors*

CHAPTER 3: NARCISSISM IN CHILDHOOD

- *How self-centered behavior appears once children enter school*
- *Effects on sibling dynamics and friendships*
- *Possible long-term implications if traits go unchecked*

CHAPTER 4: NARCISSISM IN ADOLESCENCE

- *Influence of peer groups and social status on teen narcissism*
- *Impact of social media and technology on teenage self-obsession*
- *Potential strategies for parents and educators to set boundaries*

CHAPTER 5: NARCISSISM IN ADULTHOOD

- *Shifts in personality traits and sense of self after the teen years*
- *Consequences in careers, friendships, and intimate relationships*
- *Why some adults struggle with deepening self-obsessed habits*

CHAPTER 6: TRAITS THAT SHAPE SELF-OBSESSED BEHAVIOR

- Detailed look at the key personality traits linked to narcissism
- How entitlement, need for approval, and lack of empathy intertwine
- Recognizing fragile self-esteem beneath the grand exterior

CHAPTER 7: EFFECTS ON SOCIAL RELATIONSHIPS

- Why constant self-focus often damages friendships and group ties
- Patterns of conflict and "drama magnets" in social circles
- How to detect one-sided connections and protect personal well-being

CHAPTER 8: EFFECTS ON FAMILY DYNAMICS

- Strain caused by narcissistic parents, siblings, or close relatives
- Implications for children's emotional development and self-worth
- Tips for setting clear limits at home and seeking outside support

CHAPTER 9: EFFECTS ON ROMANTIC PARTNERSHIPS

- Early charm vs. long-term manipulation in self-obsessed relationships
- Signs of control, jealousy, and emotional exploitation
- Coping methods, therapy options, and when to walk away

CHAPTER 10: NARCISSISM IN THE WORKPLACE

- How self-focused traits undermine teamwork, morale, and trust
- Spotting manipulation, blame-shifting, and grab for credit
- Role of HR policies and leadership training in addressing issues

CHAPTER 11: NARCISSISM IN TECHNOLOGY AND SOCIAL MEDIA

- *Rise of online platforms as stages for self-promotion*
- *Influencer culture, editing tools, and "likes" as drivers of vanity*
- *Strategies for mindful use of tech and building genuine connections*

CHAPTER 12: THE THIN LINE BETWEEN CONFIDENCE AND NARCISSISM

- *Core distinctions between healthy self-esteem and harmful pride*
- *Examples of balanced vs. extreme reactions to setbacks or success*
- *Ways to support real confidence without fueling arrogance*

CHAPTER 13: MYTHS AND MISCONCEPTIONS

- *Common misunderstandings about narcissism, such as "they always love themselves"*
- *Why subtle, vulnerable, or quiet forms of self-focus are often missed*
- *How myths block early recognition and effective help*

CHAPTER 14: SELF-ESTEEM VS. NARCISSISM

- *Deeper comparison of authentic self-worth vs. insecure showiness*
- *Methods to nurture one's self-esteem without belittling others*
- *Encouraging true growth and empathy in children and adults*

CHAPTER 15: PHYSICAL AND EMOTIONAL CONSEQUENCES

- *How narcissistic habits add to chronic stress, mood swings, and health risks*
- *Impact on loved ones—anxiety, burnout, or "secondary stress"*
- *Importance of seeking therapy, self-care, and healthy life routines*

CHAPTER 16: RECOGNIZING HARMFUL BEHAVIOR

- Red flags that show narcissism has crossed into abuse or danger
- Gaslighting, financial exploitation, and physical intimidation
- Documenting incidents, knowing legal options, and finding safety

CHAPTER 17: APPROACHES TO ADDRESS THE PROBLEM

- Therapy, boundary-setting, and empathy training as key interventions
- Adjusting workplace and family dynamics to limit damage
- Realistic goals, patience with setbacks, and acceptance of one's limits

CHAPTER 18: HANDLING A NARCISSIST

- Daily coping tips—communication tactics, self-care plans, and "safe exits"
- Keeping emotional distance, deflecting manipulation, and preserving peace
- When to step back or end a relationship for personal health

CHAPTER 19: POTENTIAL FUTURE IMPACTS OF NARCISSISM

- Possible societal trends if self-focused attitudes spread
- Effects on workplaces, schools, political leadership, and culture
- Response strategies—community-building, ethical leadership, balanced media

CHAPTER 20: REFLECTING ON SELF-OBSESSED BEHAVIOR

- Summary of key traits, effects, and tools for prevention or change
- Why balancing personal ambition with empathy is vital for healthy bonds
- Last thoughts on building respectful, supportive communities

CHAPTER 1: INTRODUCTION TO NARCISSISM

Narcissism is a word that many people hear, but not everyone understands. It refers to a way of thinking and acting where a person has an inflated sense of self. This person may feel they are more important than others or that they deserve special treatment. They might think their needs always come first and that they are above rules or limits. Narcissism can show up in small ways, such as talking about one's own achievements too often. It can also show up in bigger ways, like ignoring the feelings and rights of others. When we talk about narcissism, we are not talking about self-respect or healthy self-esteem. Those things are good and help people feel confident. Instead, narcissism goes far beyond normal confidence and becomes harmful.

One way to start understanding narcissism is by looking at a famous story from ancient times. Long ago, people spoke of a man who fell in love with his own reflection in a pool of water. He was so taken with himself that he could not look away. He cared only about his own image. In this story, the person's name was Narcissus, and his behavior helps us understand the idea of being self-obsessed. While most people are not this extreme, the story gives us a picture of what it means to be blind to anyone's needs other than our own.

Narcissism is not just a simple personality trait that someone can ignore. It can become a pattern of behavior that shapes how a person relates to others. In daily life, narcissism might show up in many forms. A person might brag about their successes all the time, even if the success is small. They might not think about how others feel. They might think that every topic of discussion should lead back to them. They might also say or do things to make sure they remain the center of attention. Some people might show these traits once in a while, but a true narcissist acts this way so often that it becomes part of who they are.

There is a difference between healthy pride and harmful self-obsession. Healthy pride can motivate a person to do their best. It can give them energy to meet goals and feel good about who they are. But harmful self-obsession is different. It makes a person lose sight of empathy, which is the ability to care about how others feel. Empathy is very important in friendships, families, and all kinds of relationships. Without empathy, a person might treat others poorly. They might not notice when they hurt someone's feelings. They might even blame others for problems they cause. When narcissism gets in the way of empathy, it creates many problems for both the narcissist and those around them.

Sometimes, people with narcissistic traits find themselves alone. Others may not enjoy being around someone who only talks about their own needs. Friends or family members might become tired of feeling ignored. At work, coworkers might grow frustrated with a person who takes credit for everything and never shares praise. Over time, a narcissist may discover that people do not want to be close to them. This can lead to conflicts, broken relationships, or even job loss. Because of these risks, understanding narcissism is important.

Many people wonder what causes narcissism. It's not easy to give a simple answer. Experts often point to several factors, including personality style, upbringing, and life events. For some people, a childhood where they were always told they were the best might make them think they should always come first. For others, a tough childhood with harsh criticism may lead them to protect themselves by acting as if they are more special than others. There can also be effects from cultural norms or social media, which reward people who show off or seek constant attention. The roots of narcissism can be complex.

You may wonder how to spot narcissism in yourself or in others. At times, you might find certain habits, such as bragging, ignoring rules, or expecting others to solve your problems, popping up in your behavior. Everyone has a moment or two of self-focus, so it is not unusual to slip into mild self-obsession. The big difference is whether it becomes a major part of who you are. True narcissists find it hard to turn off these traits. Even if told to stop, they may not care. Their sense of being above others might drive them to believe they do not have to listen.

It's important to note that some degree of self-care and self-respect is healthy. We should feel good about our abilities. But when our self-focus becomes so strong that we cannot see others, that is when problems start. Narcissism can push people into conflict, harm relationships, and leave them feeling empty inside. It can cause them to lose real connections. These real connections are important for a happy life. Over time, the lack of deep bonds with others can become painful. Even if a narcissist does not show it, deep down, they might feel lonely.

Sometimes, people may ask if narcissism is the same as being confident. Confidence is having faith in one's abilities. A confident person knows they can do something well, but they do not think that makes them better than everyone else. Narcissism, on the other hand, goes beyond confidence. A narcissist wants constant approval, wants to be seen as the top person, and shows little care for how others feel. They might lie or exaggerate to look good. They might take advantage of people. They might even pretend to be caring if it helps them get what they want. This difference between healthy confidence and selfish pride is key to understanding narcissism.

Another way to tell if someone is acting with narcissism is to notice how they handle setbacks or criticism. A confident person might feel disappointed when they fail at something, but they can usually handle it. They might try again or learn a better way. A narcissist, however, might refuse to accept blame. They might lash out at others. They might say the problem was unfair or that someone was out to get them. They cannot stand to think that they did something wrong. This way of handling problems can become a cycle of blame and hostility, which often leads to more trouble.

Some people with narcissistic traits can still appear charming. They might have good manners or treat people nicely at first. But over time, the self-obsessed side appears. They might try to control conversations or situations so they always look good. They might push others aside to stay in the spotlight. When conflicts arise, their response can be very harsh. They may not feel sorry, and they might even become angry if asked to consider someone else's view. This can leave loved ones feeling confused, because they saw a nice side at first and did not expect the person to act this way.

It is helpful to know that narcissism is not always simple to spot. Many people can have a few narcissistic tendencies here or there. To say a person is a narcissist, you would expect to see these traits appear again and again. It affects their friendships, family life, and more. They may have an inflated idea of their talents, claim they are more skilled than they really are, and ignore facts that do not agree with their view of themselves. When this pattern repeats, it can lead to lots of stress and unhappiness. People close to them might try to explain why such behavior is harmful, but often, the narcissist will not listen.

Those who study the mind, like psychologists, have tried to classify narcissism. It can be broken down into different forms. Some people show grand narcissism, where they are openly boastful, like a flashy show-off. Others show vulnerable narcissism, where they might act shy or fearful on the outside, but still think they should have special treatment. They can feel upset if they do not get constant praise or feel ignored. Both forms are self-centered, but they look different on the outside. A person might shift between types, too. There is no simple rule that says one form is fixed.

Understanding narcissism can help people protect themselves from harm. It can also help them see if they have any of these traits. If you recognize these patterns in your own life, it might be wise to reflect on them. The first step in dealing with any pattern is to notice it. If you see it in a friend or family member, that knowledge can help you understand why they act in a certain way. You might see that their constant boasting or need for attention is not a short-term phase. Instead, it may be a lasting part of their personality. With this knowledge, you can choose how to respond and whether you want to keep close ties with that person.

In the chapters that follow, we will look at how narcissism appears in different stages of life. We will talk about how children might show hints of narcissism, how teens develop self-obsessed habits, and how adults learn to live with or without these traits. We will also examine the impact on social relationships, family life, romantic bonds, and even the workplace. By taking a closer look, we can see the bigger picture of how a self-obsessed mindset can grow and affect others over time.

A big reason why narcissism matters is because it can hurt people who interact with the narcissist. Loved ones might feel that their thoughts or emotions do not matter. Friends might feel used or ignored. Coworkers might see an unfair environment. Classmates might notice one student always hogging attention in group projects. Over time, this can create stress and sadness. A narcissist might not notice or might even deny it. In their mind, they are only doing what feels natural to them—shining a light on their own needs and wants. But for everyone else, it becomes draining.

Even so, people with narcissistic traits can also be interesting or creative. They might have big goals and do big things. They might excel in fields where boldness is rewarded. But if they do not learn how to share credit, work well with others, and respect boundaries, their success can be short-lived.

Relationships are a big part of any person's life. If those connections are broken, a person may end up lonely, even if they have many awards or a big following.

In summary, narcissism involves a strong focus on oneself in a way that blocks out care for others. It can make a person seek constant praise and approval. It can lead to a cycle of blame and defense. It can create friction in families, friendships, and workplaces. When this behavior goes unchecked, it can grow stronger, causing even more damage to connections. Understanding it is the first step to seeing what might be happening in certain people or even ourselves. It does not mean every person who acts selfish now and then is a narcissist. We all have self-centered moments. But a pattern of such behavior across many parts of life is a sign of something deeper.

We will expand on these ideas in the next chapters. We will talk about how narcissistic traits begin to form. We will look at how they might show up in children who demand all attention or in teens who want to be stars among their peers. By looking at these early roots, we gain a clear idea of how narcissism grows. From there, we will see how it affects adults and how it can appear in families, romance, and the workplace. Each chapter will focus on a different aspect of narcissism, so that we can fully understand how it works in day-to-day life. Once we see the patterns, we are better able to respond and, if needed, make changes.

Remember, narcissism is not just a word for someone who loves themselves. It is about an ongoing pattern of self-importance, a lack of empathy, and a push to feel superior. Not everyone who seems proud is a narcissist. It is the intense, lasting traits that matter. By the end of this book, you will have a clearer view of what these traits look like, where they come from, and the effects they can have. You will also learn ways people can address such behavior and how to handle it when it appears in someone close to you.

Narcissism is a topic that many people find tricky. But with the right knowledge, we can see it for what it is: a mindset that places one's own reflection above everything else. It is like a mirror that a narcissist cannot stop looking into. They may miss out on the real world outside that mirror. This can hurt both the narcissist and the people around them. The goal here is to bring clear understanding of narcissism so that you can see it when it appears, know what it means, and perhaps even help lessen its negative impact on your own life or someone else's.

CHAPTER 2: EARLY SIGNS OF NARCISSISTIC BEHAVIOR

In this chapter, we will look at how narcissistic traits can show up early in a person's life. Sometimes, we think of narcissism as a problem that shows up in older children or adults. But, in some cases, the seeds of this self-obsessed behavior can be seen when a child is very young. Knowing these early signs can help parents, caregivers, teachers, and others understand how certain habits form and possibly how to guide a child toward healthier ways of thinking.

When a child is very small, it is normal for them to focus on their own needs. Babies cry for food, comfort, or rest. They cannot take care of themselves. Toddlers can also be demanding. They are learning to communicate, and they do not fully understand other people's feelings. But as children grow, they start to learn empathy. They realize that other people have emotions and that it is not all about them. They might share toys or comfort a friend who is upset. This is a normal part of growing up. When these steps toward empathy do not happen, or when a child displays patterns of selfishness beyond what is typical for their age, we might see signs of narcissistic behavior starting to form.

One early sign can be an extreme need for praise. All children like to be told they did a good job, but some may want it constantly. They might become angry or sad if they do not get praise. They might talk about their successes over and over, no matter how small. This behavior on its own does not prove narcissism, but it can hint that a child is placing too much weight on being admired. They might struggle to accept that other children also do well or that adults cannot always pay full attention to them.

Another sign could be a refusal to follow basic rules without throwing a big tantrum or trying to argue their way out of trouble. Many children test limits. This is typical for growing minds. But if a child seems to believe that rules do not apply to them at all, it might signal that they feel they are above others. They may show anger or shock that someone is telling them "no." They might ignore warnings or blame others for mistakes. Again, each of these behaviors alone does not prove narcissism, but the pattern can signal a deeper issue.

You might also see a child who is overly concerned with appearances or status, even from a young age. For instance, they might always talk about having the best clothes, the newest toy, or the most exciting vacation. They might look down on others who do not have the same items. In many cases, children learn this kind of behavior from their environment. If they see parents or loved ones putting too much value on material things, they might copy that. Or they might see it on TV or online, where people show off fancy items. When a child becomes obsessed with looking better than others or always tries to gain attention, it can be an early sign of narcissism.

Some children also show a habit of controlling conversations or demanding that they get the spotlight. A child might interrupt others, shift every discussion back to themselves, or show disinterest whenever someone else is talking. If you notice this happening often—way more than what is usual for their age—it can suggest a growing self-centered mindset. Young children might do this at times, but if it becomes a pattern, it might need attention.

When these behaviors start showing up, it is important to remember that children are still learning. Many kids may act in self-focused ways without growing into narcissistic adults. What matters is how these behaviors are handled. If adults around the child do not set limits or do not help the child learn empathy, the behavior might get stronger. If the child learns that they can get what they want by being pushy or by showing no concern for others, they might keep doing it. On the other hand, if parents or caregivers point out when the child is being unfair, help them see others' feelings, and reward kind actions, it might prevent these early traits from turning into a bigger problem.

Sometimes, a child who shows early signs of narcissism might also have trouble making real friends. They might try to dominate playtime or brag until other children feel uncomfortable. They may act upset when other kids want to play a different game. They might show little concern if another child is hurt or sad. When the child's peers start to avoid them, the child may become angry, confused, or even try harder to force friendships on their terms. This cycle can lead to a difficult social life, with the child feeling lonely but still not learning how to be considerate of others. Early intervention from adults can help the child build better habits.

There can also be an influence from the parenting style the child experiences. If a parent praises the child non-stop or never lets the child face the results of their mistakes, the child might grow up thinking they are perfect. They might come to believe they never do wrong. If a parent always blames others for the child's errors or scolds teachers or coaches who try to give feedback, the child might see that as proof they are above rules or criticism. On the other hand, if a parent is very harsh and always criticizes the child, the child might use self-obsessed behavior as a shield. They might act like they are perfect to cover up deep feelings of not being good enough. So, either extreme parenting style can push children toward narcissistic traits.

Experts say that early detection and balance in how we treat children can help steer them away from narcissism. For example, teaching children to share, to wait their turn, and to see that other people's feelings matter can give them a more balanced view of themselves and others. Letting them fail in small ways and learn from mistakes can also help. When a child sees that they can recover from errors, they learn humility and resilience. If a child is never allowed to fail or is never told when they are wrong, they might keep seeing themselves as flawless.

Teaching healthy empathy is also important. Parents and caregivers can talk to children about how to recognize emotions in others. They can ask questions like, "How do you think your friend felt when you took that toy?" or "How would you feel if that happened to you?" These small talks can build a child's sense of care for others. Over time, children who learn empathy are less likely to become consumed by self-importance. They can still have confidence, but they also see that others matter.

It is worth noting that some children naturally show more self-focused behavior than others. They might have strong personalities or big goals. That alone is not a bad thing. It can turn into a problem if they also show a lack of concern for others' rights or feelings. A child who is driven but still caring is different from one who is driven at the expense of everyone else. Recognizing this distinction is key. When caring adults spot trouble signs, they can step in.

At school, teachers might notice a child who always tries to be the leader, always wants the best seat, or always talks over classmates. The child might show little respect for group rules. If teachers see this, they can encourage group activities that require cooperation. They can point out respectful behavior and explain why it is good. They can gently redirect the child if they are hogging the spotlight. Over time, these actions can help the child see that while they might have strengths, they also need to be fair and kind.

Some signs of early narcissism can also appear online if a child is allowed to use social media at a young age. They might always try to post content that highlights themselves and ignore or belittle others. They might demand likes or comments, and feel upset if they do not get them. Of course, social media can encourage self-focus in many people, not just children. But in a child with an already self-obsessed style, it can push them further in that direction.

Parents may also notice that a child with narcissistic traits might have trouble handling feedback. For example, if a child is drawing pictures and a friend suggests adding a different color, the child might explode and say, "You're just jealous," or something similar. They might blame the friend for being mean. They might refuse to consider that their friend was trying to be helpful. This inability to handle feedback can be a clue of deeper problems. If this pattern repeats, it can affect the child's progress in school, sports, or creative activities.

It is important to state again that not all of these signs automatically point to full-blown narcissism. Children go through many stages. They can have phases of being extra focused on themselves, and then they grow out of it. It is the repeated pattern over time that raises concern. If a child keeps showing these traits in different settings—home, school, sports teams—and does not change even when guided, it might indicate a more lasting style of thinking.

Some families might ignore the signs, hoping the child will grow out of it. Others might think their child is just special or gifted. While positive thinking about a child is fine, ignoring harmful behavior can let narcissistic patterns become stronger. If a child reaches the teen years with a strong sense of entitlement and little empathy, it can be even harder to correct later. That is why noticing these signs early can be helpful.

In some cases, a child might start therapy if their behavior is causing big problems at home or at school. Therapists can help the child learn how to see others' points of view, handle rules, and respect boundaries. Parents can also learn new ways to interact with the child so that they do not unintentionally reward self-obsessed actions. For instance, they might learn to avoid always giving in to the child's demands and instead encourage small acts of kindness. This might take time, and there can be pushback, but consistent guidance can make a difference.

Children who show early narcissistic behaviors might still have good qualities. They can be smart, talented, or funny. The key is to help them see that those qualities should not overshadow the value of kindness, fairness, and respect. The world does not revolve around one person, and learning this lesson is vital for healthy development. As these children grow, they will interact with more people. If they never learn empathy, they risk damaging relationships. They might face anger or rejection from peers who do not appreciate their self-centered ways. They might also face more serious conflicts if they cannot accept authority or follow rules.

By understanding these early signs of narcissistic behavior, caregivers can pay attention to the day-to-day attitudes of a child. Rather than guessing why a child is bossy or demanding, they can see that it might be part of a larger pattern that needs attention. This chapter does not mean to label every challenging child as a narcissist. Instead, it aims to point out red flags that could signal a bigger issue. Looking at these signs can help those in charge of a child's well-being find the right balance. Children can learn that they are unique and able to achieve great things, while also recognizing that other people have worth, too.

A balanced approach is often the best path. Praise the child for real achievements, but also guide them when they are unkind. Let them know it is not okay to mock others or to ignore rules. Show them how to share and how to listen. Talk about the feelings of people and characters in books or movies. This helps them practice stepping into someone else's shoes. Over time, these small steps can guide a child away from harmful self-obsession and toward a healthier view of self and others.

In the next chapter, we will look at narcissism in childhood more deeply. We will talk about how it grows once children leave their toddler years and enter school. We will also see how external influences like parents, media, and social circles can shape a child's self-view. By watching for these signs and acting early, there is a better chance of redirecting a child's thinking before narcissism becomes deeply rooted. Children's minds are flexible. If we give them the right lessons at the right time, we can help them avoid a harmful pattern of self-obsession.

CHAPTER 3: NARCISSISM IN CHILDHOOD

Childhood is often seen as a time for growing and learning in many areas. It is when children start to understand rules, form friendships, and figure out how the world works. During these early years, patterns of behavior can become strong and remain in place as a child grows older. In some cases, children can develop self-centered habits that go beyond normal childhood behavior. These habits can become signs of narcissistic thinking.

In the previous chapter, we discussed early hints of narcissistic behavior in very young children. Now, we will look at how those hints can grow or change once a child is out of toddlerhood and attending school. This stage is important because children begin to spend more time with peers, teachers, and other adults. They learn new skills, take on greater responsibilities, and gain new ways to see themselves and others. If a child leans toward self-obsession, these years can either help fix the problem (if addressed properly) or make it stronger (if ignored or encouraged).

Peers and the Impact on Self-View

Once children enter school, they meet classmates who might have different skills, talents, and backgrounds. These differences can be a chance for healthy social growth. Children learn to share, wait their turn, and get along. They also learn that others can excel at certain tasks while they themselves might excel at different ones. This process should teach children that not everyone can always be in the spotlight. Over time, children come to see that success and failure happen to all of us.

But a child with narcissistic tendencies might ignore these lessons. They might refuse to give credit to classmates who perform well. They might look for any chance to outshine others. In group projects, they might insist on deciding how tasks are done or claim most of the praise for the group's achievement. If teachers or adults do not step in, this mindset can cause friction. Classmates might avoid this child or argue with them.

In many cases, the child who displays these self-focused behaviors may not realize how they push others away. They might think they are only showing pride in their work. However, the difference is that they may do so in a way that ignores the feelings of others. They might mock a friend's lower test score, brag nonstop about their own, or act like no one else matters. Over time, these choices can block real connections from forming.

Family Influences and Daily Home Life

School life is just one factor. A child's family plays a huge role in how their self-view grows. Some parents might feed a child's sense of being special beyond normal praise. Constantly telling the child they are better than others, protecting them from the smallest problem, or never letting them face the results of poor decisions can give the child a false sense of superiority. The child might grow to believe they can do no wrong. They may also come to expect that everyone around them will treat them with the same level of approval.

On the other hand, some families might ignore a child's feelings altogether. This can cause a child to develop an inflated self-focus as a kind of shield. They might decide that the only way to feel safe is to think they are above criticism. If they do not believe in their own "special" value, they might feel worthless. So, they may put on a front of being all-important to hide deep fears. Both extremes can feed narcissistic styles.

Siblings also affect how children form their sense of self. A child might feel the need to be the best among their brothers or sisters. They might compete for the most attention, the highest marks, or the best sports results. In many families, sibling competition is normal and can be healthy if it teaches children how to handle winning and losing. But in a household that encourages self-obsession or fails to teach respect for each other, the child might develop harmful views. They might see their siblings as threats to their spotlight or grow resentful if they must share space and resources. These feelings, when unchecked, can add to a child's self-centered habits.

Role of Teachers and Other Mentors

Teachers, coaches, and mentors can have a big impact on a child's mindset. They can help guide a child away from extreme self-centeredness by recognizing effort, teamwork, and fairness. When a teacher praises a student not only for a good grade but also for helping others, it sends a signal that caring behavior matters. In classrooms where teachers reward cooperation—like taking turns speaking, showing kindness, or working in pairs—the child can see that success involves more than personal achievement.

However, if teachers focus only on top grades or highlight one star student too much, children with self-focused traits might see that as proof of their special position. They might think, "I must always be first, or I am nothing." A balanced approach is best. That means praising good outcomes while also valuing team spirit and empathy. Coaches can do something similar on sports teams by rewarding not just the star player who scores, but also the teammate who gives a good assist or supports others.

If a child continues to show bossy or rude behavior, a teacher might schedule a talk with the child's parents. They can share examples of how the child behaves in class, how it affects others, and what changes might help. If parents react by defending the child no matter what, it can reinforce the child's sense that they can ignore rules. But if parents and teachers work together, the child learns that the same expectations for respect and empathy exist at home and at school.

Media and Cultural Influences

Children are often exposed to different forms of media: TV, videos, online content, and more. Some of these influences might highlight stardom or placing oneself above others. Certain shows might glamorize a character who always wants attention, or reward shallow traits like showing off fancy items. A child who is leaning toward narcissism might be drawn to such messages. They might think the best way to be happy is to get endless approval from others.

At the same time, there can be positive media influences that show kindness, friendship, and respect. It is helpful if a child's parents or guardians talk to them about these differences. They can point out which behaviors in shows are helpful and which ones are harmful. This does not mean lecturing the child, but instead discussing what it means to be a good friend, a caring family member, or a fair leader. When children are guided to think critically about what they see, they can develop a more balanced outlook.

Development of Empathy

Empathy involves feeling concern for others and trying to see the world from another person's point of view. During childhood, empathy can grow if a child is encouraged to talk about feelings and understand how actions affect other people. One simple way to do this is by asking a child questions like, "How do you think your friend felt when you refused to share?" or "What would you want someone to do for you if you were sad?" These questions can help children pause and think about someone else's experience.

For a child who leans toward narcissistic thinking, empathy may not come naturally. They might be more focused on how to keep themselves happy or how to stay in the spotlight. If adults do not step in, these habits can keep growing. The child may begin to see other children as tools to get what they want or as threats if they also want attention. Over time, this can damage the child's ability to form healthy friendships.

Helping a child see beyond their own needs is not always simple, but it can be done through daily conversations and real-life examples. Praising small acts of kindness can reinforce the idea that caring about others is worthwhile. Letting children help with simple tasks—like feeding a pet or giving out snacks to siblings—can also build responsibility and a sense that other living beings matter. Every small step counts, and these lessons can shape a more balanced child.

Handling Criticism and Disappointment

Children who grow up with a strong self-focused view often struggle with any form of criticism or negative feedback. If a teacher says, "You made a mistake on this assignment," or if a coach says, "Try a different strategy," a self-obsessed child might lash out or make excuses. They may blame the teacher for not explaining things better. They might blame teammates for a lost game. They might refuse to own their part in any mistake.

Learning to handle normal disappointments is important for all children. It helps them become resilient and flexible. If a child never learns this lesson, they could keep dodging blame and pointing fingers at others. In time, this can cause people around them—classmates, teachers, friends—to lose patience. The child could find themselves isolated or stuck in a pattern of clinging to an image of being perfect. The more often this pattern repeats, the more deeply it becomes part of the child's identity.

Parents and teachers can help by showing the child that mistakes are a normal part of learning. Instead of reacting harshly, adults can say something like, "Everyone makes mistakes sometimes. Let's see how we can fix it." This helps the child realize that being wrong once in a while does not change their value. It also encourages them to face problems and work on solutions, rather than hiding behind blame or excuses.

Different Expressions of Self-Obsession in Childhood

Narcissistic behavior in children can show up in different ways:

1. **Bossy Leadership:** The child might insist on being in charge all the time, ignoring or shutting down ideas from peers.
2. **Excessive Bragging:** They might talk nonstop about their achievements or toys, hardly letting others speak.
3. **Manipulation of Others:** They might twist facts to make themselves look good, or trick classmates into doing their chores or homework.
4. **Extreme Reactions to Criticism:** They might melt down if a parent or teacher points out even a tiny mistake.
5. **Lack of Genuine Friendships:** Their relationships might revolve around power or control, rather than mutual respect and care.

Each child might show one or more of these patterns. Some children might switch between them, depending on the situation. Recognizing these tendencies does not mean labeling a child as a hopeless case. Rather, it is a signal that the child might need extra help in learning how to relate to others and see themselves in a fair and realistic light.

Social Challenges and Outcomes

A child who keeps acting in a self-focused way can face many social challenges. Classmates might leave them out of games or group projects. They might not be invited to birthday parties if they are known for hurting others' feelings or taking all the credit. Teachers might grow tired of the constant demands. Over time, these reactions from others can make the child even more defensive or upset. They might say it is everyone else's fault, seeing themselves as the misunderstood star of the story.

If this continues, the child could move through school with few close friends. They might group with kids who have similar habits, forming a clique that puts others down. Or they might end up feeling lonely if no one wants to put up with their behavior. The child's academic or extracurricular progress might also suffer if they refuse to cooperate in group tasks or refuse to accept feedback. These problems can get worse as the child grows, making them more likely to enter adolescence with a shaky foundation for healthy self-esteem.

Early Intervention and Guidance

The good news is that childhood is often a time when behaviors can still be guided in a healthier direction. If parents, teachers, and other caring adults notice these patterns, they can step in. This might include:

- **Clear Boundaries:** Telling the child when a behavior is not acceptable. For example, "It is not okay to interrupt every time your friend speaks."
- **Respectful Consequences:** If the child does something hurtful, they might lose a privilege or be asked to fix what they did wrong. This teaches them that actions have effects.
- **Encouragement of Empathy:** Asking how they think their actions make others feel. Suggesting ways to be kind or helpful to friends and siblings.
- **Open Communication:** Talking about achievements in a healthy way. Saying, "I'm proud of you for doing well, but remember your friend also worked hard."
- **Praise for Teamwork:** Notice and reward the child when they show cooperative behavior. For instance, if they share a toy with a sibling or help a classmate, give them a compliment or thank them.

It takes time for children to shift their mindset. Some children might resist, especially if they are used to always getting their way. They might test limits to see if adults will give up. But consistent guidance can begin to reshape how they think about themselves and their place in the group.

Signs that More Help Might Be Needed

Sometimes, a child's self-obsessed behavior is so strong that basic home or school guidance is not enough. The child might refuse to listen to parents or might disturb the classroom to a serious degree. In these cases, families might consider getting help from a counselor or mental health professional. A trained specialist can look more closely at why the child has these behaviors. They can provide strategies to handle them. Therapy might include play-based sessions, where children learn about sharing, empathy, and handling frustration in a safe environment.

Parents might also learn how to change the way they respond at home. If parents discover that they unintentionally reinforce the child's narcissistic thinking, they can learn new ways to set boundaries. This might involve saying, "I know you are upset that you didn't win this time, but it's important to try again. How else can we practice so you get better?" instead of swooping in to shield the child from all disappointment. Over time, therapy and improved family habits can help a child build a healthier sense of self and others.

Building Healthy Self-Esteem Instead of Self-Obsession

One big concern for parents is how to keep a child's confidence high without encouraging self-obsession. This is possible. Children should feel proud of what they do well, and they should recognize their strengths. The difference lies in how they see those strengths. A balanced child can say, "I'm good at math, and my friend is great at music. We both have something to offer." A self-obsessed child might say, "I'm better than everyone at everything, and if I'm not, then it's their fault."

Adults can model this balanced mindset by acknowledging their own mistakes and praising the abilities of others. For example, a parent might say, "I burned the cookies today, but I'll try again tomorrow," or, "Your cousin is really good at painting, and you're really good at building structures. You can learn from each other." When a child hears these views, they learn that it is normal to have both talents and flaws. They also learn that it is good to notice what other people do well.

In addition, teaching a child to appreciate teamwork can build healthy self-esteem. Working on group tasks or playing on team sports can help them see the value of combining everyone's strengths. If they see that a teammate's pass led to a score, they might begin to realize that success is not just about one person. Over time, these experiences can help a child adjust their view of themselves and the group.

Long-Term Outlook

Childhood is a formative period. It offers many chances for healthy growth and also for patterns that can lead to problems in later life. If narcissistic tendencies are not addressed, they may become stronger as the child faces more complex social environments and bigger personal challenges. On the other hand, if these tendencies are dealt with through proper boundaries, empathy-building, and consistent feedback, the child might develop a more balanced sense of self.

A child who learns that they can be proud of their gifts but also appreciate others is less likely to harm relationships. They will also be better equipped to handle setbacks in school, sports, or friendships. While no child can be perfect, a child who has a fair sense of self and respect for others is better prepared to manage the ups and downs of life without constant drama or blame.

As we move to the next stage—adolescence—the demands on a young person increase. They face new social pressures, changes in their body, and a growing need for independence. If a child enters those teen years with a strong self-obsessed mindset, they might face greater conflicts. That is why it is so vital to address narcissistic traits in childhood, before they become too set in place. Early guidance, thoughtful teaching, and a caring family environment can help a child move toward healthier ways of relating to the world.

In the end, narcissism in childhood does not mean a child is certain to remain that way. With attention, patience, and clear boundaries, many children can grow out of self-focused habits. They can learn to balance pride in their own accomplishments with genuine appreciation for others. By doing so, they stand a better chance of forming meaningful connections, finding real success, and going forward with a stable and realistic sense of who they are.

CHAPTER 4: NARCISSISM IN ADOLESCENCE

Adolescence is a time when a young person begins to take steps toward becoming an adult. During these years, teenagers face new responsibilities, social pressures, and a shifting view of themselves. Their bodies change, their friendships can shift, and they start to question the rules set by parents or caregivers. All these changes can either lessen or worsen any narcissistic traits they may have developed earlier.

Some teens handle these years by exploring their interests, making friends, and gradually learning to stand on their own. Others might struggle with feelings of insecurity, social anxiety, or a need to prove themselves. For a teen with narcissistic tendencies, this stage can heighten their self-obsession or cause them to behave in new ways to maintain the spotlight. In this chapter, we will look at how narcissism can appear during the teen years, what factors influence it, and how it affects relationships with peers and family.

Shifts in Peer Groups and Social Status

A large part of a teen's sense of self comes from their peer group. Friends often shape how a teen dresses, talks, and acts. Teenagers who long for attention might see their social circle as a way to get approval. They might try to become the center of attention at parties or online, hoping to look important or interesting. Some teens do this through humor or style, while others might show off expensive items or brag about experiences.

A teen with strong narcissistic traits may not just want to fit in; they might aim to stand out above everyone else. They might brag constantly about their achievements or exaggerate their experiences to seem more impressive. They could act as if they are always right, putting down anyone who disagrees. This can lead to conflict, especially if their peers see through the bragging or get annoyed by the constant self-focus.

Social media also becomes more relevant in adolescence. Teens might post pictures, stories, or videos in the hope of getting likes and comments. For a teen who already craves admiration, social media can become a stage for showing off. They might carefully craft their posts to look perfect or highlight their talents. If they do not get the response they want, they might feel angry, depressed, or blame others for "not appreciating them enough." This cycle can feed narcissistic thinking, as the teen equates online approval with self-worth.

Changing Family Dynamics

As teens push for independence, conflicts with parents or caregivers can become more frequent. A teen with narcissistic tendencies might argue that house rules are unfair or beneath them. They might refuse to do chores, claiming they have more important things to do. They might expect parents to meet their every need without giving back. In normal teen development, some rebellion is typical as they figure out their own identity. But a self-obsessed teen may take it further, acting as though they are above any guidelines or responsibilities.

This can strain family relationships. Parents who try to set limits might face anger or dismissal. Siblings can feel overshadowed if the narcissistic teen hogs attention with loud or dramatic behavior. Sometimes, the teen may even play family members against each other to get what they want, possibly lying to create conflict. If parents do not stand firm, the teen's sense of being above rules can get stronger.

At the same time, some parents unknowingly support narcissistic traits by never letting their teen face consequences. For instance, a parent might repeatedly defend the teen's rude behavior to teachers or coaches, or might shower them with expensive gifts whenever the teen demands it. Though this might seem like support, it can send the message that the teen's wants matter more than respect or empathy for others.

Romantic Relationships and Self-Image

Adolescence is often the time when teens start to explore dating or romantic connections. For a teen with narcissistic traits, these relationships might serve mainly to boost their ego. They could seek out partners who give them nonstop praise. They might lose interest if the partner begins to expect a fair give-and-take. In some cases, the teen may show controlling behaviors, wanting the partner to revolve their life around them.

This can lead to heartbreak or conflict. The partner might feel used or ignored. At the same time, the narcissistic teen might not see any problem with their actions. They might feel entitled to attention and admiration, believing that their partner should cater to their every need. If the relationship ends, the teen might quickly move on without showing genuine remorse. Or they might become angry and blame the partner or outside forces for the breakup.

In a healthier teen relationship, both people learn about communication, respect, and boundaries. But for the self-obsessed teen, these lessons can be ignored. They might focus on their own emotional highs and lows, paying little attention to their partner's feelings. Over time, this can hurt their ability to form stable relationships in adulthood unless they learn to see others as more than a source of approval.

Pressures of Academics and Activities

Many teens face pressure to excel in school or in extracurricular activities such as sports, music, or clubs. For a narcissistic teen, these can be arenas to show off. They might chase recognition at all costs. They could boast about their grades or athletic achievements. If they do not succeed, they might make excuses or find someone else to blame. They might accuse teachers of not liking them or coaches of favoring other players, rather than admit they might need more practice or effort.

Because of this, the teen might not learn important lessons about perseverance and teamwork. Instead, they keep shaping their view of themselves around praise and achievement. If they do fail, they might have an extreme reaction, possibly lashing out at anyone who points out what went wrong. In group activities, they may try to control the outcome so that all credit goes to them. This can create tension with classmates who want a fair share in the group's success.

Parents and teachers can step in by reminding the teen that learning involves trying, failing, and trying again. If the teen is only focused on bragging rights, they are missing out on the true process of growth. Encouraging a teen to reflect on mistakes in a calm way can help them see that it is normal not to be perfect. Over time, this might ease some of their self-obsession, though it may take patience and repeated reminders.

Identity and Self-Reflection

Teenagers often spend time asking themselves, "Who am I?" They might experiment with different styles or friend groups. This process can help them find genuine interests and values. For a narcissistic teen, self-reflection can be clouded by a need to see themselves as special or superior. They might dismiss any traits that do not fit their view of being perfect or above others.

If a teen does not allow themselves to see their weaknesses or learn from mistakes, they might struggle to form a clear and realistic identity. They may cling to a fantasy version of themselves, one that is always right, always admired. When reality clashes with this fantasy—such as failing a test, losing a competition, or being rejected by a peer—they might react strongly or seek to blame someone else.

Working on self-reflection can help. This might include writing down thoughts in a journal or talking with a counselor about real strengths and weaknesses. If a teen can learn that having flaws or making mistakes is part of being human, they can start to see themselves more honestly. This does not always come easily, especially if they have grown up receiving only praise or excuses for poor behavior.

Substance Use and Risk-Taking

Adolescence is also a time when some teens might try new experiences, including risky ones. A teen with a strong sense of self-importance might feel immune to consequences. They might believe, "I can handle anything," or, "Rules don't apply to me." This can lead them to experiment with substances or break rules more often than peers. They might also chase thrills because they like the attention that comes with being daring or bold.

Risky behavior can become a way for them to stand out in their social group. They might brag about how they stayed out all night, broke a rule, or did something dangerous. However, these choices carry real dangers. They could face legal problems, damage their health, or harm relationships. Because narcissistic teens often blame others, they may not learn from close calls. They might say, "It wasn't my fault," or "No one else understands," and continue.

Adults in the teen's life can guide them by setting clear limits and not ignoring signs of risky behavior. If a parent, teacher, or coach sees that the teen is heading toward harmful actions, early intervention is key. That might mean removing certain privileges or seeking counseling. Consistency is important. If the teen sees that boundaries change based on their excuses or smooth talk, they may keep testing limits.

Cyberbullying and Online Conflicts

During adolescence, online interactions become a bigger part of life. Teens message each other, post on social media, and join various online communities. A teen with narcissistic traits may use these platforms to boast, create drama, or tear others down. For instance, they might post insults toward classmates or spread rumors, all to feel powerful or to keep the spotlight on themselves.

This behavior can be very harmful. It affects not only the teen doing it but also the targets of the negative posts. Cyberbullying can lead to serious emotional harm. The narcissistic teen might not care or might say it is just a joke. They might not see the real pain they cause, or they might not care enough to stop if it keeps them at the center of attention.

Schools now often have rules against cyberbullying, and some communities have laws to deal with it. If a teen is caught, they may face real consequences, including suspension from school or legal problems. Parents who spot signs of cruel online posts or messages need to address it right away. They can talk with the teen about the damage done and, if needed, limit their online access. Ignoring this behavior often allows it to grow.

Possible Paths Away from Self-Obsession

Although adolescence can heighten self-centered traits, it can also be a period for change. Teens can still learn new ways of seeing the world. They are at a stage where they can reflect on themselves and gain insight if given the right tools. Here are some steps that might help a narcissistic teen move toward a healthier approach:

1. **Encourage Volunteering or Helping Roles:** When teens engage in tasks that help others—like community service or tutoring younger kids—they can discover new feelings of connection. They see that giving can be rewarding in itself.
2. **Teach Them to Accept Feedback:** This might involve guiding the teen to look at a poor grade or a missed shot in a game as a chance to improve. Show them that growth often comes from honest self-examination, not from ignoring reality.
3. **Limit Social Media Use:** If online posts are fueling narcissistic habits, parents might set a schedule or boundaries for social media. This can reduce the teen's constant need for online approval and drama.
4. **Model Respectful Behavior:** Teens learn a lot by watching. If they see parents or adult figures listening to others, admitting mistakes, and showing kindness, they might start to copy that. Conversely, if adults around them act self-centered, it reinforces their own narcissistic style.
5. **Encourage Real Friendships:** Helping the teen foster close, genuine friendships can reduce their need to chase shallow approval. Good friends will challenge them, support them, and also set healthy limits on unacceptable behavior.

When Professional Help May Be Needed

Some teens have such extreme self-obsession that regular parenting and school efforts do not seem to help. They might grow more defiant, manipulative, or even engage in harmful acts. If a teen's behavior is causing severe issues at home or in school, or if they show signs of other mental health concerns like depression or anxiety, it might be time to seek a counselor or therapist.

Therapy can offer a safe space for the teen to explore why they feel they must always appear perfect or above others. It can also help them learn better coping skills for stress, peer pressure, and emotional ups and downs. Family therapy can help parents and siblings learn how to set firm rules and handle conflicts in a consistent way. While therapy is not a quick fix, it can open the door to lasting change.

The Road Toward Adulthood

Eventually, teens become adults. They may start working or attend college, move out of their parents' home, and take on new responsibilities. If a teen never learned to see beyond their own wants, they might face bigger problems in adulthood. Jobs demand cooperation, and relationships demand respect. A narcissistic adult can struggle to hold a job if they refuse to work as a team or handle feedback from bosses. They might also jump from one relationship to another, blaming each breakup on the other person.

On the other hand, if a teen receives the right guidance, they can learn to manage their self-obsession and form a balanced identity. They can discover that being admired is nice, but it is not everything. They might find hobbies and goals that fulfill them in genuine ways, without needing to show off. They might form real friendships and loving relationships based on mutual care and trust.

It is important to remember that adolescence is often a bumpy time, even for teens without narcissistic traits. Most teens are dealing with many changes at once. This can lead to strong moods, arguments, and shifts in behavior. But the teen with narcissistic traits may handle these challenges in a more extreme way. Recognizing the signs and intervening can prevent problems from growing worse.

Conclusion

Narcissism in adolescence can be complex. These teens might show off, seek constant admiration, and lash out when criticized. They might have shallow relationships and focus too much on social media praise. They may manipulate friends, see themselves as above rules, or blame others for their own failures. All of these behaviors can harm their social life, family connections, and sense of self-worth in the long run.

However, adolescence also offers a chance for new understanding and growth. Many teens mature during these years, learn from mistakes, and gain empathy for others. If parents, teachers, and mentors are willing to guide them—by setting consistent boundaries, encouraging empathy, limiting unhelpful online habits, and offering healthy outlets—these teens can learn to soften their self-centered approach.

In the chapters ahead, we will look at narcissism in adulthood and explore how these traits play out in various settings. We will see how they affect careers, friendships, and romantic relationships. Understanding how teen narcissism shifts into adulthood will give us a wider view of how this behavior can shape a person's life for better or worse. By looking at each stage carefully, we can see how important it is to address self-obsession early and keep guiding individuals toward healthier ways of seeing themselves and others.

CHAPTER 5: NARCISSISM IN ADULTHOOD

Adulthood is a period when people often take on serious responsibilities. They may have jobs, families, or community roles. It is also a time when personality traits become more solid. If someone has grown up with a strong sense of self-focus, they may carry those patterns into the adult world. For some adults, their self-centered habits might become less obvious if they learn skills like teamwork and respect. But for others, these habits can grow stronger, causing problems at work, in families, and in friendships.

In this chapter, we will look at how self-obsessed behavior appears in adults. We will explore its effects on personal and professional life. We will also consider why some adults show these traits more strongly than others, and what can happen when they do not address their behavior.

Workplace Behavior

A job environment is often the first place where adult narcissism becomes clear to others. In many workplaces, people must collaborate, take direction from bosses, and consider the needs of clients or customers. A self-obsessed adult may have trouble following instructions. They might believe their way is always the best way. They could also expect special treatment from their boss or coworkers, such as flexible rules or perks that no one else gets.

If they manage to get a leadership role, they might use that power to boost their own status rather than help the team. For instance, they could take credit for group successes while blaming coworkers if projects fail. They might ignore rules if they think those rules slow them down. Over time, this can create tension in the office, as colleagues may feel taken for granted.

When conflicts arise, a self-obsessed adult might handle them poorly. Instead of looking for a fair solution, they might insist that they are right. They could react with anger, belittle others, or withdraw completely if they feel blamed. This kind of reaction can damage trust among teammates, making it difficult to work together again in the future. Because of this, narcissistic adults may switch jobs often or struggle to move up the career ladder in a healthy way.

However, some adults with a self-centered style can succeed if they work in fields that reward boldness and showmanship. For example, certain industries value people who are very good at self-promotion. A narcissistic adult might excel in those areas, at least for a while. Yet, if they do not learn to treat others fairly, problems will likely appear eventually. Few workplaces function well when one person constantly demands special treatment or attention.

Friendships in Adulthood

Friendships among adults can also reveal self-obsessed traits. Adult friendships are often built on mutual help and shared experiences. Friends might trade advice about personal problems, cheer each other on at milestones, or provide support during hard times. A person with strong self-focused behavior may treat friendships more like one-way streets. They could expect their friends to listen to their stories or needs but show little interest when the roles are reversed.

Over time, friends might become frustrated if the narcissistic adult only calls or visits when they want something. They might notice that this friend never shows up to support them in return. Eventually, a once-friendly group might drift away, leaving the self-obsessed adult confused or resentful. They might blame others for "abandoning" them without seeing that they played a role in driving people away.

Adults who behave this way can move from one group of friends to another, constantly hoping to find individuals who will shower them with admiration. They might get angry or sad if they discover that friends have lives that do not revolve around them. Some may keep a few close companions who tolerate their behavior, but these friendships can be strained. Because adults have many responsibilities—work, family, personal goals—they often have little energy for a friend who demands nonstop attention.

Romantic Partnerships

In a romantic setting, self-obsession can lead to major conflicts. A person with these traits might expect their partner to praise them often or comply with their wishes. They could get upset if their partner tries to voice a different opinion. They might also become jealous if their partner spends time with friends or family, feeling that all attention should belong to them.

Early in a relationship, the self-obsessed adult might seem charming. They could use smooth talk or lavish displays to win over a partner. But as time goes on, the partner might notice signs of manipulation or emotional pressure. The narcissistic adult might make the partner feel guilty for having personal needs. They might also pick fights to regain control when they feel ignored.

Such a relationship can become unstable. The partner might feel lonely, hurt, or worn out. They might walk on eggshells to avoid triggering anger. Over time, they may realize that a balanced give-and-take is missing. Sometimes, the partner stays in the relationship, hoping the narcissistic adult will change. Other times, they may decide to leave if the situation becomes too stressful or hurtful. For the self-focused individual, this outcome might reinforce their belief that others are at fault. They might jump quickly into a new relationship, repeating the same cycle.

Family Dynamics

In many families, adults must play roles such as spouse, parent, or caregiver to older relatives. These roles require patience and empathy. When someone has strong self-focused tendencies, they might find these tasks more difficult. A narcissistic parent might demand admiration from their children or push them to achieve things that reflect well on the parent. They might ignore the child's own interests or struggles. This can harm the child's emotional growth, as they may feel they exist to please a parent who rarely shows genuine warmth.

In married life, a narcissistic partner might insist that household decisions revolve around them. They could dismiss their spouse's concerns or do little to share chores. If conflicts come up, they may look for someone else to blame. Over time, the other family members might feel stressed or powerless, unsure how to manage the demands. Extended family gatherings can also be tense if the narcissistic adult tries to control the event or starts arguments over minor issues.

Despite these problems, some narcissistic adults can appear pleasant in public. They may save their self-centered behavior for behind closed doors. This can be confusing to relatives who see a charming face in social settings but experience a completely different person in private. Family members might feel guilty for resenting someone who appears so likable to outsiders.

Financial Choices and Responsibility

Money matters can also highlight adult narcissism. A self-obsessed person might spend beyond their means to keep up a grand image. They might buy expensive clothes, cars, or gadgets to impress others. They could use credit cards without planning how to pay them off. Over time, this can lead to financial trouble, debts, and even legal concerns. In some cases, the person expects a spouse, parent, or friend to bail them out each time.

If someone tries to bring up the need for budgeting, the narcissistic adult might become defensive or insulted. They might refuse to accept any blame for poor money choices. They could say, "I deserve the best," or accuse others of trying to hold them back. This attitude can block them from learning to handle money in a mature way.

In group settings where money is shared—like a household budget or a community fund—a narcissistic adult may create mistrust. They might misuse funds or insist on spending resources for their personal gain rather than the group's benefit. When confronted, they may deflect or deny wrongdoing, creating confusion and anger among people who had hoped for fair use of resources.

Handling Stress and Setbacks

All adults face challenges: job losses, health problems, or unexpected costs. Most people learn to adapt, seek support, and find ways to move forward. A narcissistic adult, however, might see challenges as unfair attacks on their perfect self-image. They could blame others, claiming that someone sabotaged them. They might refuse help from friends or experts because they believe they know best, or they might see asking for help as a sign of weakness.

When they do fail, they may rewrite the story to protect their pride. For example, if their business goes under, they might say it was entirely because the market was bad or an employee betrayed them. They may avoid owning up to any errors in planning or leadership. As a result, they lose the chance to learn from mistakes.

In personal stress, such as dealing with an illness, a self-obsessed adult might demand constant care and attention. They may not realize how emotionally draining it can be for the people around them. They might also turn minor health concerns into big dramas, seeking sympathy and admiration for their "strength" in hard times. This can exhaust loved ones who want to help but also need the person to face reality and responsibilities.

Social Circles and Group Settings

Beyond workplaces and families, adults often have social circles like clubs, neighborhood groups, or faith communities. In these settings, a narcissistic adult might try to gain control of events or push their own views at meetings. They could take on roles for the status it brings, not necessarily to serve the group. If they succeed, they might dominate discussions or use the group's resources to spotlight themselves.

When group members notice this behavior, tensions may grow. People might attempt to remove the narcissistic adult from a leadership role or confront them about fair treatment. In response, the self-obsessed adult could accuse others of jealousy or sabotage. They might cause further drama, hoping to keep the center of attention. If they fail to remain in control, they might leave that group and look for a new one to impress.

Sometimes, the narcissistic adult finds a loyal following, especially if they are charismatic. They may gather people who admire their confidence or who fear speaking against them. This can create a social bubble where the self-obsessed adult's views go unchallenged. However, these bubbles often burst when the demands become too high or people see the truth of the situation.

Online Personas and Image Management

With the rise of digital platforms, many adults share parts of their lives online. For a self-obsessed person, the internet can be a powerful tool to gain followers and reinforce their sense of being special. They might post only carefully chosen images, brag about accomplishments, or craft stories that make them appear flawless. Each like or comment can serve as a boost to their ego.

However, this can lead to an even bigger problem: living for online approval. If posts do not get the reaction they expect, they might feel angry or worried. They could spend large amounts of time trying to enhance their digital presence instead of building real connections. Over time, the gap between their online persona and their real life can grow wider. Friends, coworkers, and family might notice the difference and question the honesty of that image.

Sometimes, self-obsessed adults use online platforms to attack people they feel have slighted them. They might write negative posts, send harsh messages, or start rumors. This behavior can damage reputations and harm relationships. It also fosters more conflict, which can make the narcissistic adult feel like they are still the main focus, even if in a negative way.

The Role of Therapy and Self-Awareness

Not all self-obsessed adults remain that way forever. Some reach a point where they see the downsides of their behavior—maybe they lose a job, face a breakup, or realize they have no genuine friends left. In these moments, they might become open to seeking help. Therapy or counseling can provide a space for them to learn about empathy, self-reflection, and healthier ways of relating to others.

However, not all narcissistic adults agree to therapy. Some refuse to believe they need help. Others might start therapy but resist any suggestion that they change. Progress usually requires a willingness to admit mistakes and a true desire to respect other people's needs. This can feel uncomfortable for someone who has spent much of life feeding a self-image of perfection. Yet, if they stick with the process, real improvements can happen over time.

Self-awareness is a key factor. An adult who begins to ask, "Why do I always need praise? Why do conflicts follow me wherever I go?" is taking the first step. With guidance, they can see how their actions affect others and how they can build healthier relationships. This does not mean they lose confidence. It means they learn to balance self-respect with genuine respect for others.

Effects on Mental and Physical Well-Being

Adults who remain stuck in narcissistic patterns can face mental and physical stress. Constantly needing admiration can create anxiety, especially in social or professional situations. They might worry about slipping up and losing the admiration they rely on. If conflicts are frequent, the stress level can rise. Over time, stress can harm physical health, leading to sleep troubles or issues with blood pressure.

Feelings of emptiness can also appear. External praise might not fill deeper emotional needs. The person may chase bigger goals or more attention, but each new success loses its thrill quickly. They may feel isolated because they do not have real emotional ties. All of this can impact mood, leading to anger or sadness that they may not fully understand.

Loved ones also feel the stress. They might become anxious trying to please the narcissistic adult or keep peace in the household. Over time, they can experience burnout. This can strain the bond between the narcissistic adult and those around them, creating a cycle of loneliness and repeated conflict.

Paths Toward Healthier Behavior

It is possible for adults with self-obsessed traits to make changes. Here are some ways they might start:

1. **Honest Feedback:** Friends, family, or coworkers might need to speak up. While this can cause tension, it can also help the adult see that their actions have negative effects. Sometimes, a strong wake-up call is needed.
2. **Setting Boundaries:** If people around the narcissistic adult learn to say "no" and stick to it, the person might realize that old tactics of blaming or

sweet-talking no longer work. This can push them to reflect on their behavior.
3. **Professional Counseling:** A trained therapist can help the narcissistic adult explore why they feel the need to be the center of attention. Therapy can teach new habits, such as listening actively and taking responsibility.
4. **Focus on Shared Goals:** In work or family settings, having common aims can teach the value of cooperation. If the narcissistic adult sees a clear benefit in collaborating, they might become more open to the idea.
5. **Learning Empathy Skills:** Workshops or group sessions that teach empathy can guide adults in seeing life from another's viewpoint. This might not be an instant fix, but it can gradually expand their thinking.
6. **Accountability Partners:** Having someone (like a close friend or coach) point out times when the narcissistic adult slips back into old patterns can help the adult stay aware. Over time, these gentle reminders can shape healthier behavior.

Conclusion

Narcissism in adulthood is more than just a quirk. It can damage careers, friendships, and families. Adults with these traits may struggle to keep stable jobs or relationships because they often place their own needs above all else. Though they might appear confident, they can be deeply insecure, relying on praise to feel worthy.

If unchecked, these traits can lead to a cycle of conflict, job hopping, broken relationships, and regret. But there is hope for change, as long as the person is ready to face the truth about their behavior. Therapy and steady support can help them develop empathy, respect, and realistic self-confidence. By doing so, they gain a chance to form more genuine bonds, succeed at work without trampling others, and build a life that is not driven only by the need for admiration.

In the next chapter, we will look at the specific traits that shape self-obsessed behavior. By learning about these traits, we can better understand how narcissism grows and why certain people become more self-centered than others. Having that knowledge will help us see new ways to address the problem, whether in ourselves or in someone close to us.

CHAPTER 6: TRAITS THAT SHAPE SELF-OBSESSED BEHAVIOR

Every person is a blend of traits. Some traits, like kindness or flexibility, can help build strong relationships. Others, like jealousy or fearfulness, can cause issues if left unchecked. When a person develops a self-obsessed outlook, certain traits stand out more than others. In this chapter, we will explore the specific traits that often show up in narcissism, how they shape behavior, and why they can be so powerful. We will also consider how people can grow more aware of these traits to manage them in healthier ways.

Inflated Sense of Self-Importance

One key trait is a strong belief that one is more special or important than others. This might show itself in thoughts like, "I deserve better treatment," or "My problems matter more." While it is normal to value oneself, an inflated sense of self-importance goes beyond that. It can push a person to ignore other people's needs or expect praise for basic actions. They might feel angry or hurt if they do not get the recognition they think they are owed.

This overblown self-image often leads to conflict. Suppose a group is working on a project. A person with this trait might expect to lead, even if someone else is more qualified. When they cannot take the lead, they might become resentful or try to undermine the true leader. In relationships, they may refuse to see their partner as an equal, insisting on more rights or power than the other person. This can strain even the strongest bond.

Constant Need for Approval

Many people like to hear "good job" or get a compliment from time to time. But a self-obsessed individual often craves approval in an ongoing way, like a thirst that cannot be quenched. They might fish for praise by showing off achievements or by telling stories that highlight their skills. If others do not applaud, they feel overlooked or disrespected. This can lead to moody behavior, anger, or attempts to force attention.

Why is this trait so strong? It might stem from insecurity. Deep down, the person may fear they are not truly special. They look for others to confirm their worth, but no amount of praise is ever enough. Each "good job" feels nice for a moment, but soon they need the next one. This cycle can prevent them from finding stable self-esteem, tying their sense of value to what others say.

Low Empathy

Empathy is the capacity to share or understand another person's feelings. It allows us to see that others have thoughts and emotions that matter. In a self-obsessed person, empathy is often weak. They might find it hard to care about problems that do not affect them directly. Even if they can act sympathetic when it benefits them, it might be more of a show than a genuine concern.

With low empathy, conflicts can become bigger. If a friend shares a tough experience, the narcissistic person might interrupt with their own story or brush off the friend's feelings. They could forget birthdays or big events in other people's lives because they do not see why those events are significant. Over time, this lack of empathy can leave people around them feeling unimportant or used.

Entitlement

Entitlement is the feeling that one automatically deserves certain things or treatment without earning them. For instance, a narcissistic individual might think they deserve top pay at work, even if they lack the experience for that position. Or they might believe they should be allowed to break rules if it suits them. When others do not comply, they can feel wronged or enraged.

This sense of entitlement can show up in smaller everyday ways as well. For example, they might skip lines, take the largest share of a shared meal, or drop last-minute requests and expect immediate help. These actions reveal an assumption that everyone should adjust to their desires. People who interact with them might give in to avoid fights, but this only makes the sense of entitlement stronger over time.

Manipulativeness

Manipulation means using indirect or dishonest methods to get what one wants. A self-obsessed person might twist facts, spread half-truths, or play people against each other. They could charm someone with compliments and kindness, only to demand favors later. If confronted, they might deny what they did or act innocent. Their goal is to stay in control, even if that means harming trust or honesty.

In personal relationships, manipulation can be very damaging. Loved ones might sense that something is off but cannot always prove it. Over time, this behavior can erode confidence, leaving partners or friends confused about who is right. In workplaces, manipulation might involve taking credit for others' work, creating rivalries, or telling lies to a manager to get a promotion. This can harm team spirit and lead to resentment.

Fragile Self-Esteem Underneath

A surprising trait in many self-obsessed people is a fragile sense of self-worth below the surface. They might appear confident, but deep down, they may be anxious about being exposed as flawed. This can explain why they react so strongly to any hint of criticism. Even mild feedback can feel like a threat to their entire image.

This hidden fragility can create a push-pull pattern. On one hand, the narcissistic individual pushes to be admired. On the other hand, they feel uneasy because they fear that their "perfect" image might crack at any moment. This can lead to defensive behavior, angry outbursts, or running away from situations where they might be judged. People around them might find it puzzling that someone who acts so sure of themselves can also seem so insecure when challenges arise.

Lack of Accountability

Taking responsibility for one's actions is a key part of mature behavior. A self-obsessed person often avoids accountability. They might blame others or claim that the situation was out of their control. If they miss a deadline, it is the boss's fault for not reminding them. If they say something hurtful, they might argue the other person is "too sensitive." This pattern can appear repeatedly, causing those around them to lose trust.

Without accountability, it is hard for a person to learn from mistakes or grow. They might leave a string of failed projects, broken relationships, or unresolved conflicts behind them. Each time, they explain it away as the fault of someone else. This keeps them from noticing what part they played in these troubles and how they can act differently in the future.

Grand Goals and Unrealistic Plans

It is not unusual for ambitious people to set high goals. But a self-obsessed individual may set huge goals without a clear or realistic plan to reach them. They might claim they will be famous, become a CEO overnight, or otherwise surpass all competition in record time. While big dreams can be motivating, the narcissistic person might ignore practical steps or advice. They just expect success to come because they see themselves as special.

When reality sets in, they may give up quickly or blame external factors for not meeting their target. They might also move from one dream to another without following through on any of them. Friends or family could become worn out by constant talk of grand ideas that never materialize. This pattern can lead to frustration and wasted opportunities.

Impulsivity

Impulsivity involves making quick decisions without thinking them through. Though not all self-obsessed people are impulsive, many can show this trait. They might suddenly decide to quit a job, buy an expensive item, or change life plans for reasons that do not make sense to others. In their view, it feels like an exciting or bold move. But they may not weigh the long-term results.

This impulsivity can lead to financial trouble, damaged relationships, or other setbacks. When things go wrong, the narcissistic person may not see how their rushed choices led to the outcome. Instead, they may scramble to find someone to blame or an excuse to explain away the problem. This keeps them from slowing down and learning to plan carefully.

External Influences

While many of these traits come from internal beliefs, the outside world also plays a role. Certain environments can strengthen self-obsessed behavior. For example, if a workplace rewards only those who are loud or pushy, a narcissistic person might keep climbing the ladder. If a family never corrects a child's selfish actions and only offers praise, that child might grow up believing they can do no wrong. Media can also glamorize self-centered figures, making it look normal or even admirable to demand all eyes on you.

However, external influences can also help curb these traits. A supportive community, a fair-minded boss, or honest friends can guide a person to see the impact of their actions. Over time, strong social norms that value empathy and cooperation can teach a self-obsessed person to adapt. The question is whether they are willing to learn from these influences.

Why These Traits Form

Researchers have offered different ideas on why some people develop these specific traits. In some cases, a person might have grown up with too little attention, causing them to overcompensate in adulthood. In other cases, they might have been told they were better than others from a young age, leading them to adopt an inflated self-view. Traumatic experiences, inconsistent parenting, or cultural factors can also shape someone's sense of self.

It is important to note that having one or two of these traits does not mean a person is fully self-obsessed. Many people can show hints of entitlement or a desire for approval. The difference is that a truly narcissistic individual shows many of these traits over a long period and across different parts of life—family, friends, work, and more.

Recognizing These Traits in Yourself or Others

Sometimes, it can be hard to see these traits in yourself. Self-reflection might be clouded by defense mechanisms. If people start pointing out certain behaviors—like always needing praise or getting angry at small criticisms—it could be a sign to look deeper. Asking close friends or family for honest feedback can be helpful, though it takes courage to hear what they say.

Recognizing these traits in someone else is also not always simple. A self-obsessed person can be charming at first, hiding some of the more toxic habits. Over time, though, patterns start to emerge. You might notice they never admit fault, they fish for compliments a lot, or they break rules without remorse. Keeping track of these signals can help you decide how to handle that relationship.

Addressing the Problem

If someone realizes they have these traits, what can they do? The first step is to become open to the idea that change is possible. They might seek therapy to dig into root causes. They can practice empathy by listening more and making a point to ask questions about others. They can learn to pause before making decisions, think about the outcome, and consider how others might feel.

For friends or family dealing with a self-obsessed person, setting boundaries can reduce stress. If they always show up expecting you to solve their problems, you might calmly say you have your own tasks to handle. If they constantly fish for praise, offer genuine feedback instead, including both strengths and weaknesses. Over time, these actions might prompt the person to see that their usual methods no longer work.

Possible Outcomes if Traits Remain Unchecked

When these traits remain strong and unchallenged, they can lead to ongoing turmoil. Friendships might fade away, jobs may come and go, and personal savings could be lost. A person might reach middle age or older adulthood feeling empty, unable to keep healthy bonds. Some turn bitter, convinced the world did not appreciate their greatness.

In more serious situations, a refusal to learn or adapt can lead to legal problems, major debts, or deep isolation. A person might cut ties with family who tries to help, or they could burn bridges in professional circles. It is a bleak outcome for someone who likely started with normal human needs for connection and respect. By ignoring empathy, accountability, and fairness, they may lose the very things that could have given them lasting contentment.

Small Steps Toward Better Ways

Making big changes can be tough, especially for someone who has built their identity around self-obsessed habits. However, small steps can make a real difference over time:

1. **Admit the Possibility of Error:** Even if it is hard to do so publicly, they can start by telling themselves, "I might not always be right."
2. **Practice Listening:** In a conversation, intentionally focus on what the other person is saying. Ask follow-up questions instead of turning the topic back to yourself.
3. **Show Respect for Rules:** Rather than looking for ways to avoid guidelines, follow them and see how it feels to be fair.
4. **Reflect on Failures:** If something goes wrong, write down what part you played in the outcome. This can help break the habit of blaming others.
5. **Seek Honest Feedback:** Talk with a trustworthy friend, family member, or therapist. Ask them to point out moments when you seem self-focused or dismissive. Try to receive their input calmly, even if it stings.

Each of these steps can slowly reshape how a person thinks and interacts. They might discover that real confidence does not come from always appearing perfect or being on top. It comes from knowing oneself—flaws and all—and still trying to act with kindness and respect.

Conclusion

Self-obsessed behavior often grows from certain core traits: an inflated sense of self-importance, craving for approval, low empathy, entitlement, manipulativeness, fragile self-esteem, avoidance of accountability, unrealistic goals, and sometimes impulsivity. These traits do not always appear all at once, but when many of them come together and remain over time, they create a pattern we recognize as narcissism.

By looking closely at these traits, we gain insight into why some people act in self-centered ways and how it can harm their relationships and their own well-being. We also see that, in some cases, the person may be hiding deep fears or insecurities behind a mask of pride.

Learning about these traits is the first step toward dealing with narcissism—either in ourselves or in those around us. It can guide us to be more patient but also more assertive in setting boundaries. It can help us understand that self-obsession is not always a sign of true self-confidence. Sometimes, it hides fragile feelings and a fear of being seen as "less than perfect."

In the next chapters, we will look at how narcissism affects social ties, family life, and romantic relationships in more detail. We will also discuss the myths and misconceptions that surround this topic. By gaining a deeper understanding, we can respond more wisely when we meet people who display these traits—or when we notice the same tendencies in ourselves.

CHAPTER 7: EFFECTS ON SOCIAL RELATIONSHIPS

Social life is an important part of being human. We form bonds with neighbors, classmates, coworkers, and friends we meet in various settings. Most of these connections are built on understanding, compromise, and a shared enjoyment of time together. However, when a person's behavior is marked by self-obsession, these normal features of social life can break down. This chapter looks at how narcissism affects social connections, from casual acquaintances to closer friendships. We will explore the ways self-centered traits lead to conflict or isolation, how groups respond, and possible steps individuals can take to cope with or address narcissistic influences in social circles.

Superficial Charm vs. Lasting Connections

One puzzling thing about people with narcissistic tendencies is that they can seem very charming at first. They may flatter others, be entertaining, or show an exciting presence. In a social setting—like a party or a group hangout—this person might stand out as confident or fun. New acquaintances might be drawn to them because they appear self-assured or have lots of stories to share.

Over time, though, this charm can wear thin. The same person who seemed fascinating can turn out to be self-focused, interrupting others or steering every topic toward themselves. What first came across as confidence may start to look like bragging or arrogance. Friends might notice that discussions always circle back to the narcissistic individual's successes, needs, or issues, while other people's viewpoints are brushed aside. As this pattern continues, the group may feel drained.

People may still invite the narcissistic friend to events, hoping to keep the peace or because they recall the initial spark. But eventually, these relationships can remain at a shallow level if the self-focused person never shows genuine concern for others. Acquaintances might become uneasy about sharing personal stories, knowing they will receive little empathy in return. Without real mutual support, the connection cannot deepen. Many end up limiting contact, keeping interactions short and polite.

Group Dynamics and Narcissism

Narcissism can also influence the way groups function. In informal groups—like a circle of friends—a self-obsessed member might push for more attention in every conversation. If the group tries to plan an activity, the narcissistic person might insist on doing whatever suits them best. They might ignore what others want to do or turn minor disagreements into larger arguments.

This behavior can create tension. Some group members may feel angry that their ideas are never considered. Others might avoid speaking up, fearing the narcissistic friend will belittle them. Over time, a once-friendly group can lose its balance. People might start having side discussions to complain about the person, but hesitate to address them directly. This cycle of frustration can continue until either the group falls apart or takes steps to fix the problem.

In more formal group settings—like clubs, volunteer teams, or community committees—a similar pattern can play out. The narcissistic member might try to take charge or undermine decisions that they did not propose. They may also refuse to do basic tasks that they see as beneath them. If they are in a leadership role, they might overlook the input of other members, claiming they know best. When confronted, they could become hostile or defensive. The other members may then find themselves dealing with repeated conflicts, or they might choose to remove the disruptive individual if the group's rules allow it.

The "Drama Magnet"

A common result of narcissism in social settings is constant drama. The self-focused individual might complain about being slighted, blow small issues out of proportion, or pick fights to draw attention. Even events that are supposed to be relaxed—like a casual dinner or a weekend meetup—can be overshadowed by conflicts they initiate. The narcissistic person might accuse others of ignoring them or not giving them the seat of honor, even if no such seat exists. They may take an offhand comment personally and use it to spark an argument.

This pattern can exhaust friends, who never know when the next explosive conflict will happen. Some might try to soothe the narcissistic person, hoping to avoid an outburst. Others might stand up to them, leading to bigger arguments. A few might quietly slip out of the friend group to escape the tension. Over time, a "drama magnet" may find themselves with fewer and fewer reliable companions. The ones who remain might stick around because they have known the person for a long time or they feel guilty about leaving them alone. But this sense of obligation can breed resentment.

Social Media Ties and Image

Social media platforms bring a new dimension to social relationships. A self-obsessed person might post frequently, sharing photos and updates that paint them in a perfect light. They could use filters, catchy captions, and polished images to gain praise. Each like or comment can feel like a short-lived boost to their self-esteem. However, the interactions often remain surface-level.

Friends and followers might notice a pattern: nearly every post celebrates the individual's own achievements or appearance. If anyone posts a different viewpoint or a critical remark, the narcissistic person might react with anger or block them. This can stifle real conversation, leaving behind only people who continue to flatter them. Over time, the person's feed can become an echo chamber with little genuine back-and-forth.

Offline, these patterns can change how people perceive the narcissistic friend. They might see them as vain or disconnected from everyday life. In face-to-face interactions, acquaintances could sense that the person is more concerned about capturing the perfect online moment than in truly engaging. This gap between the online persona and real-world behavior can weaken trust. Some friends might feel they do not know the "real" person behind all the posed pictures.

Hostility Toward Perceived Rivals

In social circles, it is natural for people to have different strengths. One friend might be skilled in sports, another in cooking, and another in art. However, a person with narcissistic traits may see anyone else's talent or success as a threat.

Instead of applauding a friend's new job or impressive performance, they might grow resentful. They could try to overshadow the friend's success by bragging about themselves. They may also gossip or spread rumors to drag the friend down.

This hostility makes it difficult for genuine support to flourish in the group. People might feel hesitant to share their own good news, knowing the narcissistic friend might respond with jealousy or negativity. In some cases, the self-obsessed individual might create small cliques, turning certain group members against each other. They might play "favorites" to keep control. This behavior can destroy group unity.

Friends who notice this pattern might try talking directly with the narcissistic individual, pointing out how it hurts group harmony. If the person cannot change or at least see the damage, friendships may break apart. People often prefer a peaceful and supportive circle rather than one filled with constant competition and put-downs.

Loneliness Behind the Mask

Although a narcissistic person can seem to have many social contacts—online followers, party invitations, or a busy schedule—their relationships may be shallow. People might invite them for a short burst of excitement, but not include them in deeper life events. Over time, the self-obsessed individual can end up feeling lonely or left out. They might notice that no one truly confides in them or asks for their help when times are tough.

Yet, they may not connect their loneliness to their own behavior. Instead, they might blame others, calling them jealous or "fake friends." This keeps them from realizing that genuine friendship requires mutual support. Without empathy and the willingness to share the spotlight, deeper bonds rarely grow. The narcissistic person may then continue searching for new circles, repeating the same pattern.

In some cases, this sense of isolation can become overwhelming. They might lash out in anger, claiming everyone else is at fault. Or they might slip into sadness, wondering why people come and go so quickly from their life. If they cannot see the cause, they remain stuck in this cycle.

The Bystander Effect

When someone with strong self-centered traits disrupts a social circle, not everyone in the group reacts the same way. Some might challenge them openly. Others might remain silent, hoping to avoid confrontation. Still others might try to maintain friendship with both the narcissistic individual and those who feel hurt by them. This varied response can create confusion and even more conflict.

In many cases, the group does not have a clear leader or set of rules for dealing with disruptive behavior. Members might feel unsure about how to address the issue. They might fear being the target of the narcissistic person's anger. Or they might worry about losing a friendship they have had for years. Because of these fears, they may do nothing, letting the negativity continue.

This situation is sometimes referred to as a bystander effect, where people assume someone else will step in. However, if everyone stays silent, the harmful behavior can become the group's "normal." Over time, tensions build until something happens that forces a major shift—perhaps a public argument, a hurtful betrayal, or an incident that draws a clear line. Then, the group must face the problem head-on or break apart.

Recognizing Patterns in Yourself

Not all self-obsessed behavior is easy to spot in the moment. A person might see themselves as simply "confident" or "outspoken." It might take repeated feedback or a painful loss of friends for them to realize their behavior is pushing people away. If you suspect that you might have some narcissistic traits affecting your social connections, it can help to look for patterns:

1. **Dominating Conversations:** Do friends rarely finish their stories because you cut in with your own points?
2. **Expecting Praise, But Not Giving It:** Do you fish for compliments but hardly ever congratulate others?
3. **Frequent Conflicts:** Do arguments seem to follow you, and do you often blame others for causing them?
4. **Feeling Angry When Others Succeed:** Do you struggle to feel happy for a friend who accomplishes something you have not?

5. **Lack of Deep Friendships:** Do people drift out of your life after a short time, leaving you with mostly casual acquaintances?

Answering "yes" to many of these questions does not mean a person is doomed. However, it can point to areas where small changes might make a big difference. Listening more, asking questions about friends' interests, and learning to cheer for someone else's accomplishments are all steps toward more balanced friendships.

Boundaries and Healthy Reactions

If you are on the receiving end of someone else's narcissistic behavior, it is often helpful to set firm boundaries. Let the person know which behaviors you will or will not accept. For example, if they constantly insult you in front of others, you might decide to leave the interaction whenever it happens. Or if they always steer conversations toward themselves, you can calmly change the subject or say, "I'd like a turn to speak."

Being consistent with these boundaries shows that you take your own needs seriously. You do not have to argue or try to "fix" the other person. Instead, you are simply stating what you will do to protect your well-being. If the narcissistic individual values the relationship, they might adapt over time. If not, they may become angry or drift away.

In group settings, communication is key. Other members might feel the same frustration you do. Talking openly—while avoiding personal attacks—can reveal that many people are unhappy with the same behavior. Together, you can decide how to respond, whether that means speaking as a group, removing the person from certain group activities, or asking them to follow set rules.

Self-Care for Friends of a Narcissistic Individual

It can be stressful to keep a friendship going when the other person is primarily focused on themselves. Over time, you might feel emotionally drained. You might also question your own worth, especially if the narcissistic friend belittles your ideas or achievements. In these situations, self-care becomes important. Here are a few steps to consider:

1. **Seek Support Elsewhere:** Cultivate other friendships or join groups where you feel heard and appreciated. This gives you a sense of balance and reminds you of your value outside the difficult friendship.
2. **Set Realistic Expectations:** A self-obsessed person may not suddenly become empathetic. Hoping for a radical transformation can lead to repeated disappointment. Accepting smaller positive changes (or none at all) can help you cope.
3. **Practice Assertive Communication:** It might feel easier to avoid conflict, but speaking clearly about what you need can be freeing. For instance, "I'd like to finish my thought before you jump in," or "That comment was hurtful to me."
4. **Know When to Step Back:** If the relationship becomes too draining or toxic, it might be time to limit contact or even end it. This can be a painful choice, but sometimes it is needed to maintain your own well-being.
5. **Consider Outside Help:** In extreme cases, talking to a counselor or therapist can help you sort through the emotional effects of a friendship with a narcissistic person. They can offer strategies tailored to your situation.

Making the Most of Group Potential

Although a narcissistic individual can harm social harmony, groups can also be places where positive change starts. Sometimes, seeing others display kindness and fairness can influence the self-obsessed person to behave better. If they respect certain group members, they might pay attention when those members lead by example. Over time, consistent fair treatment and group standards might rub off on them.

This will not happen overnight, and it is certainly not guaranteed. But strong, supportive social circles that value cooperation and open communication can at least minimize the damage of self-centered behavior. People who might have left the group may decide to stay if they see that everyone is committed to a respectful environment.

Social Growth and Possible Change

For some, the negative results of broken friendships and social exclusion eventually become hard to ignore. They may realize that nobody wants to share good news with them, or that their invites to gatherings have dried up. Such a wake-up call can push them to reconsider how they engage with people. This might lead them to reflect on their own behavior or even seek professional help.

Change, if it comes, usually starts with small steps. Perhaps they begin by listening more, interrupting less, or showing genuine interest in someone else's day. They might learn to contain their frustration when another person gets attention. Although these actions can feel uncomfortable at first, they lay the foundation for more authentic bonds.

Friends who see these changes can offer gentle encouragement. Praise for real progress—like, "I really appreciated how you listened to me yesterday"—can reinforce better habits. Over time, a person who was once very self-focused may find more balance. They discover that social life is much richer when it is not all about them.

Conclusion

Social relationships give us fun experiences, support in hard times, and a sense of belonging. But for someone with strong narcissistic traits, interactions become stages for seeking admiration or control. What starts as charm can fade into conflict, drama, and eventual isolation. Friend groups may crumble or adapt to manage the tension. At the same time, the self-obsessed individual might feel lonely, blaming others instead of recognizing the impact of their own actions.

Even so, not all is lost. People can learn to set boundaries and practice self-care, maintaining their own well-being in the presence of a demanding friend. Groups can talk openly, decide on fair rules, and try to keep an atmosphere of respect. In some cases, the narcissistic individual might see the negative outcomes of their ways and begin to shift, learning to share space and attention.

CHAPTER 8: EFFECTS ON FAMILY DYNAMICS

Families are unique. They can provide support and closeness that we do not find anywhere else. At the same time, family relationships are often complicated by old patterns, strong emotions, and shared history. When narcissistic traits show up in this setting, the effects can be profound. Conflicts might simmer for years, parents might push children to feed their ego, siblings could become rivals, and tension can overshadow what might otherwise be a loving environment. In this chapter, we will examine how self-obsession influences family dynamics, looking at everything from parent-child relationships to the way extended relatives handle narcissistic behavior.

The Narcissistic Parent

One of the most significant ways that narcissism appears in families is through a parent who has self-centered traits. A parent holds authority, sets rules, and usually shapes the emotional atmosphere at home. When they are narcissistic, they might use the child to fulfill their own needs rather than focusing on the child's development. For example, they could demand excessive admiration from their son or daughter, expecting constant praise for everyday tasks. They might also ignore or dismiss any feedback that suggests they are not perfect.

In some cases, the narcissistic parent might live through their child's achievements, pushing them to excel so that the parent can brag. The child's grades, talents, or successes become a reflection on the parent's worth. If the child fails or falls short, the parent might react with anger, shame, or emotional withdrawal. This can create a lot of pressure for the child, who may grow up feeling they must constantly please the parent to earn love.

Additionally, a narcissistic parent may not respect the child's individuality. They could dismiss the child's interests or opinions if those do not align with their own. Over time, the child might learn to hide their true self, fearing disapproval or punishment. This can stunt emotional growth, as the child does not get the space to explore their own identity in a safe way.

Sibling Dynamics

Siblings in a family with a narcissistic parent (or sibling) might develop complicated relationships among themselves. If the parent shows clear favoritism toward one child—praising them excessively while criticizing the others—resentment and rivalry can grow. Even if the favored child does not encourage this dynamic, the other siblings might feel ignored or belittled. In some families, one child becomes the "golden" child, and another becomes the "scapegoat." The scapegoat might receive blame for anything that goes wrong, regardless of actual fault. This role assignment can carry into adulthood, affecting how siblings relate to each other long after they leave home.

If the narcissistic individual is a sibling rather than a parent, the tension can take a different form. A self-obsessed brother or sister might always try to dominate family discussions or events. They could insist on having the best bedroom or the most expensive gifts. They might mock or belittle other siblings to stay in the spotlight. Parents who do not intervene may accidentally encourage this behavior, leading to ongoing fights and an environment of competition rather than support.

Emotional Costs for Children

Children who grow up in a home with a self-obsessed parent or sibling often face emotional challenges. They might learn that their own feelings and needs are unimportant. For instance, if a child tries to share a personal struggle, the narcissistic parent or sibling might brush it off or change the subject to themselves. Over time, the child might stop talking about their problems, leading them to feel lonely or misunderstood.

These children can also develop confusion about boundaries. A narcissistic family member may violate privacy, read diaries, or make big decisions for someone else without asking. If the child protests, the narcissistic person might laugh at them or claim they have no right to personal space. Such actions can cause the child to feel insecure or powerless at home. Later in life, these same children might struggle to set healthy boundaries in other relationships because they never saw it modeled.

Some children learn to placate the narcissistic individual, becoming "people-pleasers." They might focus on smoothing over conflicts and keeping everyone calm to avoid outbursts. While this might reduce arguments short-term, it can come at the cost of the child's own well-being. They might hide their true opinions, assume all blame, or do whatever it takes to keep the peace.

Spousal Interactions

If one spouse or partner in a household is highly self-focused, the other partner may find themselves in a challenging situation. They could feel that their own emotions and goals are overshadowed by the narcissistic spouse's demands. For example, a self-obsessed partner might expect constant praise for minor efforts, such as putting away dishes or mowing the lawn. If they receive any form of critique, they might lash out or turn the conversation around so the partner feels guilty.

Money decisions can also cause friction. The narcissistic spouse might spend family funds on flashy items or personal hobbies without discussing it. When confronted, they might deny wrongdoing or say they deserve the money because of their "special" status. This can strain finances and lead to arguments about accountability.

In some families, the non-narcissistic partner tries to keep things stable for the children. They might go along with the narcissistic spouse's demands or present a unified front to avoid confusion for the kids. Over time, however, this takes a toll on the partner's mental health. They may feel trapped, exhausted, or unsure how to break the cycle. If they do challenge the narcissistic spouse, they might face anger or emotional manipulation, leaving them isolated or fearful.

The Extended Family Environment

Narcissistic behavior can also create tension at wider family gatherings, such as holiday meals or reunions with grandparents, aunts, uncles, and cousins. The self-obsessed individual might try to control the schedule, pick arguments over seating arrangements, or steer all conversations toward their own accomplishments. If relatives do not give them the attention they crave, they might show frustration by sulking or storming off.

Sometimes, extended family members do not see the bigger picture if they interact only briefly. They might think the narcissistic relative is just confident or outspoken. But those who have spent more time with them may feel uneasy and try to avoid direct contact. This can lead to subtle divides in the family. Some might side with the narcissistic person out of fear or because they believe their version of events, while others try to maintain distance.

Over time, these patterns can turn joyful family traditions into tense gatherings. The narcissistic member might show up late, disrupt planned activities, or create conflicts that overshadow any shared enjoyment. Many relatives, worn out by the drama, could stop attending or reduce how often they visit.

Parenting Styles and Passing Down Traits

A vital issue with narcissism in families is how it might be passed down. Children watch how parents and older relatives act. If they see that self-centered behavior goes unchallenged or even gets rewarded, they might adopt the same habits. On the other hand, a child might learn from a narcissistic parent's mistakes and grow determined not to repeat them.

Still, modeling plays a big role. If a parent is constantly fishing for praise, ignoring boundaries, or blaming others, children might see that as normal. Later in life, they could replicate these actions in their own relationships. This is how some narcissistic patterns can continue across generations. However, awareness can break the cycle. If a grown child recognizes the unhealthy ways they were raised, they might seek help or read about healthier relationship patterns, working hard to give their own children a different experience.

Confronting Narcissistic Behavior at Home

Dealing with narcissism in the family is tricky because leaving is not always an immediate option—especially for children or for partners who share finances and responsibilities. Yet, families can take certain steps to respond to these challenges.

1. **Setting Clear Boundaries:** If a parent insists on reading a teen's journal, for example, the teen or the other parent can calmly explain that privacy is important. They might find a secure place to keep personal items or a locked journal. While this might anger the narcissistic parent, it sends a message that the teen has rights to personal space.
2. **Seeking Outside Perspective:** Family members might talk to a school counselor, therapist, or trusted friend to sort through confusing emotions. Sometimes, just hearing that their experiences are real and not their fault can be a relief.
3. **Creating Private Support Networks:** Siblings can support each other if one is singled out. Or they might align with a supportive relative. Feeling less alone can strengthen them. If the narcissistic individual tries to isolate them, these networks can provide an alternative viewpoint and a safe place to vent.
4. **Protecting Mental Health:** In some families, the self-obsessed member's tactics are so severe—verbal abuse, financial manipulation, or emotional threats—that professional help becomes essential. Therapy, support groups, or legal advice might be necessary to protect well-being.
5. **Limited Contact When Needed:** Adult children or other relatives sometimes choose to limit or break contact with the narcissistic family member if their well-being is at serious risk. This is not an easy decision, but it can bring relief from ongoing harm.

Managing Gatherings and Special Occasions

Family events often bring both hope and anxiety. Relatives might look forward to seeing each other but worry that the narcissistic member will cause problems. Planning can include setting ground rules or codes of conduct, such as agreeing on times, menus, and conversation topics to avoid. If the narcissistic person becomes disruptive—demanding the spotlight or insulting others—someone might gently but firmly redirect the conversation or suggest a break.

It can help to have a team approach. More than one family member can agree to calmly intervene when tension rises. For example, if the narcissistic relative criticizes someone's job, a sibling can step in with a neutral statement like, "Let's hear what they like about their work." This defuses the moment rather than giving the narcissistic person a chance to fuel conflict.

Of course, there is no foolproof plan. If the narcissistic relative is determined to cause drama, they may still find a way. However, a united front can reduce the impact and show them that the rest of the family stands together. Over multiple events, the narcissistic person may see that their usual tactics do not bring the attention or control they want.

When the Narcissistic Family Member Is Aging

Another aspect of family life is caring for aging parents or relatives. If the elderly individual has long held narcissistic traits, those traits do not simply vanish as they grow older. In fact, the stress and vulnerability of aging can make them more fearful of losing independence and thus more demanding or controlling.

Adult children trying to help might face constant complaints, criticisms, or emotional manipulation. They could arrange medical care, pay bills, or clean the house, only to hear from the narcissistic parent that they are not doing enough. Some aging narcissists pit one child against another, telling each that the other is neglectful. This can fracture sibling relationships.

In such scenarios, adult children need to set firm limits on what they can and cannot do. They might also need outside help, such as home care aides or mediators, to reduce direct conflict. It is important that they do not sacrifice their own health and finances out of guilt. Balancing compassion and boundaries can be especially challenging, but it allows adult children to provide needed assistance without enabling endless demands.

Healing and Moving Forward

While it can be hard to handle narcissism in the family, healing is possible, especially if at least some members are willing to change. If the narcissistic individual realizes the damage they have caused, they may seek professional counseling. A trained therapist can help them see why they act the way they do and how to adopt healthier patterns. This process takes time and requires genuine effort. The family can support it by encouraging honesty and acknowledging small improvements.

Even if the narcissistic family member does not change, other relatives can find healthier ways to cope. They can learn stress-management techniques, practice assertive communication, and build support networks outside the home. Siblings can strengthen bonds by treating each other with kindness and fairness. Over the years, these steps can reduce the negative effects of one family member's self-obsession.

Children who grew up in such a setting can also break the cycle as they become adults. By recognizing what happened and seeking help, they can learn to set different rules in their own households, making sure empathy, respect, and honest communication are at the forefront. They might still struggle with old wounds, but each new step offers a chance to form healthier bonds.

Conclusion

Family life can bring comfort, shared experiences, and a sense of belonging, yet narcissism can push these positive elements aside. A self-obsessed parent might demand endless praise or treat children as trophies. A sibling with strong narcissistic traits might bully others to remain in control. Extended relatives might dread gatherings, fearing the drama that unfolds when the narcissistic member is present. Over time, these patterns can leave scars on every family connection.

Yet, individuals in a family are not without choices. By setting boundaries, seeking outside help, and supporting one another, they can limit the harm. In some situations, a narcissistic parent or sibling might realize their actions are damaging the people they claim to love. That realization can mark the beginning of true change. Even if they never transform, other family members can find ways to heal, protect themselves, and foster healthier ties with relatives who are capable of empathy and respect.

Families are complex, and each one differs in how they respond. But the more we understand the impact of narcissism in the home, the better prepared we are to make choices that preserve everyone's mental and emotional well-being.

CHAPTER 9: EFFECTS ON ROMANTIC PARTNERSHIPS

Romantic relationships can bring feelings of closeness, trust, and shared understanding. Yet, when narcissistic traits enter a partnership, they can disrupt those positive bonds. A self-focused approach can show up in subtle ways at first—like one partner always steering conversations toward their own experiences. Over time, that behavior can grow stronger, making the other person feel ignored or even used. In this chapter, we will look at how narcissism can show up in romantic settings, the warning signs, and the effects on both partners. We will also explore steps someone can take if they find themselves in a relationship marked by self-obsession.

Early Stages of Attraction

When people first start dating, they often try to show their best side. They might share interesting stories, dress nicely, and treat the other person with care. For someone with narcissistic tendencies, this initial phase can be especially charming. They may go out of their way to impress the new partner by appearing confident, successful, or adventurous. They might give big compliments, plan special dates, or present themselves as very attentive. This display can sweep the other person off their feet and spark an intense attraction.

However, these early signs of excitement sometimes fade once the self-focused partner feels secure that they have the other person's attention. The compliments might stop, or the partner might begin to show less concern for what the other person thinks. The shift can be confusing. The partner who was once so caring and eager to please might become uninterested in hearing about anyone else's day. It can feel like the newness wore off, leaving behind a very different person than the one first introduced during the dating phase.

Not everyone who makes a strong effort in the beginning is narcissistic. Yet, if someone quickly flips from generous to self-absorbed after winning their partner's interest, it can be a clue that they were more invested in seeking attention than in building a real connection. Over time, this pattern might worsen, with the narcissistic partner no longer putting in effort unless they want something or feel their ego needs a boost.

Signals of Self-Obsession in a Relationship

Romantic partnerships work best when both people feel seen and appreciated. In a healthy bond, each partner listens, offers help, and tries to respect the other's goals. But when narcissism is present, certain warning signs often appear:

1. **One-Sided Conversations:** The self-focused partner might talk at length about their successes, worries, or interests, rarely pausing to ask about their partner's thoughts. If the partner attempts to share, the narcissistic individual might steer the topic back to themselves.
2. **Lack of Empathy:** When the other partner expresses feelings—such as sadness or stress—the self-obsessed person could brush it aside or respond with impatience. They might say, "You're overreacting," or "I'm dealing with worse," showing little genuine concern.
3. **Fish for Praise:** The narcissistic partner may constantly look for compliments, possibly saying things like, "You know I did great at work, right?" or "Don't I look really good today?" without returning similar warmth.
4. **Control and Manipulation:** They might use guilt or other tactics to keep their partner centered on their needs. For example, if the partner wants a night out with friends, the narcissistic person might create a crisis to keep them at home.
5. **Jealousy and Suspicion:** If the self-obsessed person sees their partner giving attention to anyone else, they can become angry or accuse them of wrongdoing. This often reveals a strong need to remain the main focus at all times.
6. **Refusal to Apologize:** In conflicts, a narcissistic partner may blame the other person or outside factors, rarely accepting responsibility. Instead of working to fix problems together, they push the blame to keep their own image untarnished.

One or two of these signals by themselves do not always prove narcissism. But when many of them appear often, they can point to a deeper, self-centered style that will likely cause long-term problems.

Emotional Effects on the Other Partner

When a person spends time with a self-obsessed partner, they might notice changes in how they feel and act. For example:

- **Eroded Self-Esteem:** Constantly trying to please someone who ignores their needs can make a person doubt their own worth. They might feel that nothing they do is good enough.
- **Stress and Anxiety:** Living with someone who might start fights or twist facts can create a constant sense of uncertainty. The non-narcissistic partner never knows when things will go smoothly or when another conflict will arise.
- **Feelings of Isolation:** If the narcissistic individual becomes jealous of the partner's friends or family, they might discourage them from having close bonds with others. Over time, the partner might feel cut off from their usual network of support.
- **Guilt and Confusion:** In many cases, a self-obsessed partner blames the other person for problems. This can lead the non-narcissistic partner to question if they are indeed at fault, creating guilt and doubt about what is really happening.
- **Emotional Exhaustion:** Always putting the other person first or trying to manage their mood can drain a partner's energy. Eventually, they might feel too tired to keep meeting the narcissistic partner's demands.

Control, Jealousy, and Possessiveness

Some self-centered partners take control to an extreme. They may track the other person's movements, check their phone, or decide which friends they can see. Though these acts can stem from insecurity, the partner uses them to maintain power. The message is: "I must be your top concern. I have the right to know everything you do."

In many of these cases, the narcissistic individual believes they deserve special privileges. They might cheat or lie but explode if they suspect their partner doing the same. This "double standard" means the narcissistic person sees no contradiction in their own behavior because they feel they are above normal rules. Meanwhile, the other partner might feel trapped. If they protest, the narcissistic person accuses them of being disloyal. If they comply, they feel they have no freedom.

Patterns of Emotional Manipulation

Emotional manipulation can take many forms in a self-obsessed relationship. One common method is **gaslighting**, where the narcissistic partner denies events or twists facts to make the other person doubt their memory or perception. For instance, if they said something hurtful a day before, they might later claim, "I never said that. You must be imagining things." Over time, this can wear down the partner's sense of reality.

Another form is **love-bombing**, where the narcissistic person showers the partner with affection, gifts, or promises right after a conflict. This sudden shift can make the partner think things are finally improving. But once the tension calms, the narcissistic person may switch back to harsh behavior. This cycle of highs and lows keeps the partner off balance, hoping each "good phase" will last.

Some self-obsessed partners also use **silent treatment** as a tactic. When angry or wanting control, they stop talking or responding until the other person begs for attention. This can make the partner feel desperate to fix the problem, even if they did nothing wrong. These manipulative methods create a climate of doubt and fear, where the narcissistic individual holds most of the power.

Conflicts and Escalation

All couples experience disagreements, but the way they handle them says a lot about the health of the bond. In a balanced relationship, conflicts can be addressed with honesty and compromise, even if emotions run high. In a self-obsessed relationship, conflicts often get amplified. The narcissistic partner might yell, threaten, or accuse the other person of being the source of all issues. They might refuse to listen or calm down.

This pattern can make any discussion feel unsafe. The other partner may try to keep the peace by backing down, fearing the argument could turn into a full-scale meltdown. Over time, the couple may stop addressing problems at all.

Instead, the narcissistic partner's wants become the unspoken law in the household. The other person tiptoes around those rules, hoping to avoid an explosive reaction. This dynamic often leads to built-up resentment, which can harm the relationship further.

Financial and Practical Concerns

Narcissistic traits can also affect money matters and daily tasks within a relationship. For instance, the self-obsessed partner might assume they have the right to decide all purchases, from major expenses like a car or house to smaller items like electronics. They might not consult their partner's opinion, seeing their own wants as the main priority. If the other partner questions these decisions, the narcissistic person could dismiss them or argue that they have a better sense of what is "best."

Additionally, one partner might be pressured into paying more bills or covering debts that the narcissistic individual creates. The self-focused partner may see this arrangement as normal, because they feel entitled to have someone else handle their responsibilities. Over time, this can cause financial strain or even lead to serious debt. The other partner may feel trapped, with their credit score or savings at risk, yet they are often blamed if they resist.

Leaving or Changing the Relationship

Not everyone who shows selfish traits in a relationship is beyond help. Some people can learn to become more considerate if they recognize the harm they are causing and choose to do something about it. Others might show no desire to change. The next steps can depend on how safe or stable the relationship is, and whether both partners agree to work on it.

1. **Self-Reflection:** If the self-obsessed partner admits there is a problem, they might go to counseling or read about ways to improve their behavior. Sometimes, seeing the impact of their actions can push them to grow more aware. However, this is usually only possible if they genuinely want to change.

2. **Couples Therapy:** When both partners are open to discussion, therapy can help them learn healthier ways to talk, set boundaries, and share responsibility. But if one partner refuses to admit any wrongdoing, therapy might not make much progress.
3. **Personal Therapy for the Affected Partner:** The person on the receiving end might seek counseling to regain self-esteem, figure out what they truly want, and learn strategies for communication. A therapist can help them decide if it is best to stay and work on the bond or to leave.
4. **Exit Strategy if Needed:** In extreme cases of emotional or physical harm, leaving the relationship might be the only safe option. This can be complicated if the couple shares finances, children, or a home. The partner might need legal advice, a safe place to stay, or support from friends and family. While ending a partnership is painful, it can sometimes protect a person's well-being in the long run.

Possible Positive Changes

Once in a while, a self-obsessed individual can transform if they understand the damage their behavior does. This shift normally requires consistent effort. They might need to learn basic listening skills—like letting their partner speak without interrupting—and to accept feedback calmly. They could also practice small acts of thoughtfulness, such as asking how their partner's day went and genuinely caring about the response. These steps can be slow, but if the self-focused partner remains committed, the relationship might become healthier over time.

For the partner who stayed, seeing honest, steady improvements can rebuild trust. They might notice changes like the narcissistic person apologizing when wrong, taking an interest in the partner's activities, or making efforts to respect boundaries. However, it is still important for the non-narcissistic partner to keep an eye on whether these actions last. Short-term changes that vanish once pressure eases could indicate a return to old patterns. Patience and consistent follow-through are key on both sides.

Tips for Recognizing Unhealthy Patterns Early

Preventing a painful, self-obsessed relationship can be easier if people learn to spot red flags early. Some actions that might be overlooked during dating or early stages could signal a larger issue:

- **They Only Talk About Themselves:** Even in casual dating, a complete lack of curiosity about your life can be a clue.
- **They Put Others Down:** Watch out for a person who constantly criticizes friends, relatives, or ex-partners. They might later direct the same negativity toward you.
- **They Avoid Responsibility:** If they always blame the boss, their past partners, or random outside factors for problems, they could have trouble owning up to their mistakes.
- **They Overreact to Minor Disagreements:** Throwing insults or storming out over small topics can mean trouble later on.
- **They Rush the Relationship Quickly:** Some narcissistic people try to lock in a partner with fast, intense gestures of love or promises, then shift behavior once they feel secure.

By noticing these warning signs, a person can pause and consider whether it is wise to invest deeper in the relationship. While nobody is perfect, patterns of selfishness or disrespect often get worse if left unchecked.

Handling Narcissism When Children Are Involved

The stakes become even higher when a couple with a self-obsessed partner has children together. The parent's narcissistic traits can affect daily interactions, from feeding routines to discipline decisions. The child might feel confused if one parent uses them as a way to get attention or competes for the child's devotion at the expense of the other parent. Over time, the child could learn to manage the narcissistic parent's moods or copy their manipulative behaviors.

In these cases, the other parent might try to shield the child by setting clear household rules, giving plenty of emotional support, and talking openly about feelings. If conflicts with the narcissistic parent escalate, the other parent could need outside help—from family therapy to legal advice. It can be tough to keep a stable environment when one parent undermines cooperation, but children do best when at least one parent gives them consistency and fair treatment.

Balancing Self-Care and Compassion

People who love someone with narcissistic traits often feel torn. They might see glimpses of kindness in their partner, remember good memories, or hope that the person can change. On the other hand, they face repeated hurtful events that wear down their emotional well-being. Balancing care for the partner with care for themselves can be challenging.

- **Set Limits:** Deciding on rules for how you want to be treated can protect you emotionally. For instance, you might calmly say you will not continue a conversation if it turns into name-calling or personal attacks.
- **Build Outside Support:** Lean on friends, counselors, or groups where you can speak freely about what is happening. Isolation often makes these situations worse.
- **Recognize Warning Signs of Harm:** If you feel threatened or unsafe, act quickly to find help. Emotional harm can be as damaging as physical harm.
- **Avoid Blaming Yourself:** A narcissistic partner might insist you are the cause of every fight, but that does not mean it is true. Remind yourself that healthy relationships do not work that way.
- **Know When to Walk Away:** If repeated efforts to fix things lead nowhere, it is okay to decide that leaving is healthier for you. This does not mean you failed; it might mean you saved your own well-being.

Conclusion

Romantic partnerships thrive on honesty, respect, and shared care. When a partner is consumed by their own reflection, those qualities can weaken. The non-narcissistic partner might feel stuck, guilty, or unloved. Over time, what should be a source of support and happiness can turn into a place of constant stress.

Yet, solutions do exist. Some self-obsessed individuals do realize the damage they cause and make changes. Others may refuse to see any fault, leaving their partner with the tough choice to stay or leave. Either way, knowing the common signs of narcissism in a romantic bond—and understanding its emotional toll—can help people protect themselves and possibly improve the situation. Seeking therapy, setting firm limits, and paying attention to one's own needs are all steps that can bring clarity and, in some cases, real change.

In the next chapter, we will look at narcissism in the workplace. Work settings involve tasks, goals, and teamwork, making it a very different environment from family or romance. However, self-obsessed behavior can still undermine cooperation and trust among colleagues. We will explore how narcissism shows up on the job, how it affects team productivity, and what can be done to address it.

CHAPTER 10: NARCISSISM IN THE WORKPLACE

Work is a major part of adult life. It is where people spend a large share of their time, form professional ties, and earn income. Many jobs require cooperation, respect for rules, and a willingness to learn from feedback. Yet, someone with narcissistic traits may clash with these expectations. They could try to stand out at all costs, hog credit for group achievements, or dismiss the ideas of coworkers. Over time, these actions can damage teamwork, reduce morale, and create tension. In this chapter, we will explore how narcissism appears in the workplace, the effects on teams and leaders, and ways that organizations and individuals can respond.

Recognizing Self-Obsessed Behavior at Work

At first glance, a coworker with narcissistic traits may seem like a real go-getter. They might appear confident in meetings, share strong opinions, and talk about how driven they are. They could even achieve early recognition if their bold style impresses managers. However, as time passes, patterns emerge that set them apart from a healthy, confident employee:

1. **Taking Credit, Shifting Blame:** They might claim ownership of a project's success when many people contributed. Conversely, they deny fault or accuse others if something goes wrong.
2. **Seeking Constant Admiration:** They may frequently bring up their past accomplishments, large or small, wanting approval from everyone around them.
3. **Difficulty Collaborating:** Group discussions can become battles if they refuse to see any viewpoint but their own. They might also interrupt or belittle coworkers who share different ideas.
4. **Avoiding Authority (Unless It Benefits Them):** They might ignore rules they see as a hindrance, yet demand that others follow those same rules. If there is a chance to curry favor with higher-ups, they will often do so while dismissing peers' input.
5. **Strong Reactions to Criticism:** Instead of seeing feedback as a chance to improve, they may become defensive or respond with personal attacks.

Not every person who shows some of these signs is fully narcissistic. Still, when several of these behaviors occur regularly, they can cause real trouble for a team.

Impact on Teamwork and Morale

A healthy workplace depends on people who can share ideas, split tasks, and trust one another. A self-focused colleague can undermine each of these elements:

- **Trust Erodes:** If someone frequently claims credit for shared efforts, coworkers lose trust in them. Over time, people may choose not to share information or suggestions for fear of being overshadowed or blamed.
- **Projects Stall:** Narcissistic individuals might reject good ideas simply because they came from someone else. This attitude can slow down creativity and innovation, as coworkers feel discouraged from speaking up.
- **Tension Increases:** Arguments can flare when the self-obsessed person demands special treatment or tries to run the show. Other team members may resent the unfairness or feel insulted by the narcissistic person's attitudes.
- **High Turnover:** In some cases, valued employees choose to leave a department or company if they cannot escape a toxic atmosphere. This means the team loses experience and must spend time and resources hiring replacements.
- **Reduced Motivation:** Feeling unappreciated or overshadowed can sap a team member's drive. They might stop putting in extra effort if they believe they will not get proper credit anyway.

These problems can spread, affecting not just one team but the entire organization. Managers may have to step in, yet they might not always see the full picture if the narcissistic employee knows how to charm them.

Narcissistic Leaders and Their Teams

Narcissism in leadership poses a unique set of challenges. A boss with strong self-focused traits has the power to hire, fire, and assign tasks. If they see themselves as above rules or believe they are always right, they might ignore the suggestions of their team. They may expect endless admiration from employees and punish those who do not deliver it.

Some narcissistic leaders do have visions that can move a company forward. They might be convincing speakers who secure big deals or bring excitement to the brand. However, problems occur if they cannot accept when they are wrong, do not credit their team, or refuse to plan realistically. Over time, employees might feel drained trying to please a boss who never shows real gratitude.

Another risk is that a narcissistic leader might foster a culture of fear. Staff may avoid questioning ideas or bringing up obstacles, worried they will be shamed or fired. Important problems can go unnoticed until they become crises. On top of that, employees may feel forced to compete for the leader's attention, resulting in a cutthroat environment rather than teamwork.

The Role of Human Resources and Policies

Well-structured workplaces have guidelines to ensure fair treatment. These guidelines often address issues like harassment, disputes, and performance reviews. When a narcissistic employee or boss ignores these rules, HR can help by:

1. **Documenting Issues:** Encouraging staff to note times and dates when rule-breaking or unfair behavior occurs. This creates a record that can show patterns over time.
2. **Clear Feedback Systems:** Performance reviews should include honest assessments of teamwork skills, respect for colleagues, and willingness to accept guidance. If someone lashes out when criticized, that becomes part of the record.
3. **Conflict Resolution Steps:** Many companies have formal ways to settle disputes, such as mediation. A third party listens to both sides and tries to reach a fair result. Narcissistic people might try to spin the story, so having a neutral mediator can help clarify facts.
4. **Training in Communication:** Some workplaces offer workshops on handling tough personalities, resolving conflicts, and giving feedback. This can help the entire team learn to deal with a self-obsessed colleague more effectively.
5. **No Tolerance for Harassment:** If narcissistic behavior crosses into bullying, discrimination, or emotional harm, HR should step in promptly. This protects employees who might otherwise feel powerless.

However, HR's ability to fix the situation may be limited if higher management does not support the needed changes. Some narcissistic bosses hold top positions, making it hard to enforce rules against them. In such cases, employees might feel stuck, and the best HR can do is document the issues or advise employees on possible paths forward.

Coping Strategies for Coworkers

If you have a self-obsessed coworker, there are ways to protect your own work environment without leaving the job:

- **Set Boundaries:** Calmly make it clear what you will and will not tolerate. For example, if they try to dump their tasks on you, say something like, "I'm already at capacity with my own workload, so I can't take on extra right now."
- **Use Written Communication:** In places where projects or tasks are assigned verbally, a narcissistic colleague might later deny any agreement. By sending follow-up emails that confirm what was discussed, you create a paper trail that reduces their chance of rewriting events.
- **Stay Professional:** Though it can be tempting to call them out in anger, it often makes things worse. Focus on job-related facts, tasks, and outcomes. Avoid letting them pull you into personal arguments or blame games.
- **Seek Allies:** You might find others in the team who have noticed the same behaviors. By sharing concerns with trusted coworkers—without gossiping or forming a hostile clique—you can confirm that you are not alone. Sometimes, a united front makes it harder for the narcissistic person to spread blame.
- **Inform Supervisors Wisely:** If the coworker's actions are harming progress, consider talking to a manager or HR. Stick to concrete examples—dates, projects, quotes—rather than vague complaints about "bad behavior." This helps management see the real impact on the workflow.

Handling a Narcissistic Boss

Dealing with a self-obsessed boss can be more delicate since they hold power over your position, pay, and advancement. Some tips include:

1. **Clarify Expectations:** Ask for detailed instructions in writing. That way, if your boss changes the story later, you can point to what was originally asked of you.
2. **Document Achievements:** Keep track of your work successes with dates, data, or emails. If a narcissistic boss fails to acknowledge your contribution, you still have evidence of your efforts. This can help in performance reviews or if you move to another department.
3. **Learn to Recognize Triggers:** Figure out what sets your boss off. For some, it might be feeling outshone in meetings, so they lash out. If possible, avoid those triggers or manage them carefully.
4. **Give Limited Praise (When Deserved):** Some experts suggest offering a bit of sincere praise when your boss does something positive. This can calm their need for recognition, making them less likely to lash out. But avoid exaggerating or flattering them on everything. Aim to keep it honest and work-related.
5. **Have an Exit Plan:** If the boss's behavior turns cruel or ends up harming your career path, you might decide it is time to leave for a healthier environment. No job is worth ongoing mental or emotional harm. Before you resign, secure references, line up new opportunities, and inform HR if any serious rule violations occurred.

Managing Narcissistic Tendencies in Yourself

Sometimes, it is not just a coworker or boss who shows narcissistic behavior. You might notice traits in yourself—like hogging credit, getting defensive when receiving feedback, or needing constant praise to feel motivated. Recognizing such tendencies in your own actions can be uncomfortable, but it also gives you the power to make changes:

- **Seek Constructive Feedback:** Ask trusted colleagues for honest input about how you handle group work. Hearing their perspective can open your eyes to areas where you could be more cooperative.

- **Develop Better Listening Skills:** Make a point to pause during team discussions and invite others to share their thoughts. Practice reflecting what they said to show you are really listening.
- **Acknowledge Mistakes:** When something goes wrong, own your part of it. Admitting errors might sting at first, but it builds trust and helps you grow.
- **Focus on Shared Wins:** Instead of only celebrating your own results (avoid that word—let's just say "highlighting your own results"), openly recognize how the team contributed. Point out what others did well. This shift can improve team morale.
- **Think Long-Term:** Remember that building stable work relationships benefits you over time. If you try to grab all the praise now but harm bonds with coworkers, it might come back to hurt you later.

By making these adjustments, you can cultivate (avoid that word—say "develop") a healthier team spirit and reduce conflict. In turn, you may discover that real collaboration feels better and yields stronger, more consistent success than chasing quick applause.

Cultural Factors and High-Pressure Fields

Some work environments might encourage narcissistic traits without meaning to. For example, a sales team that rewards only the top seller every month might push employees to step on each other to reach that top slot. High-profile fields like entertainment, sports, or politics can also attract strong personalities who aim to stay in the spotlight.

While healthy competition can motivate people, workplaces that focus only on individual triumph may create a perfect zone for self-obsessed behavior. If management never values group efforts or kindness, employees might learn that being aggressive or taking all the credit pays off. Over time, this can turn a company culture toxic. Leadership has a role here in making sure they reward teamwork, shared ideas, and honesty, not just flashy performance or the loudest voice in the room.

Virtual Work Settings

More people than ever now work from home or in remote offices, which can introduce different challenges when dealing with narcissism. Instead of face-to-face clashes, a self-obsessed person might take over online meetings by ignoring the agenda or muting others. They might send constant messages demanding attention or pressuring coworkers to respond quickly. Written communication can be twisted in new ways; for instance, they might copy the boss on every email to show off or shift blame.

In these cases, many of the same strategies still apply. Keeping records of what was agreed upon, setting boundaries on availability, and refusing to engage in personal arguments can help. When possible, team leaders can also use structured tools—like shared project boards or meeting agendas—that make it harder for one person to dominate or rewrite facts.

Possible Outcomes and Growth

When faced with a self-obsessed individual in the workplace, there is no single solution. Sometimes, clear communication and boundaries can encourage that person to work more cooperatively. Other times, they may dig in, continuing their behavior until they face consequences like poor performance reviews or removal from their role. In extreme cases, entire teams may get fed up and leave, forcing management to see the damage caused by the narcissistic employee or boss.

On the flip side, employees who handle the situation skillfully can grow more confident in conflict resolution. They learn to speak up, stand their ground, and find allies. Managers who address narcissistic behavior fairly can strengthen the entire workplace by showing that no single person's ego outweighs the group's well-being.

Organizations that embrace respect and fairness can reduce the negative effects of narcissism. They might develop recognition programs that reward both individual efforts and teamwork. They might train leaders to listen openly, share credit, and accept blame when needed. Such a culture makes it harder for a self-obsessed person to thrive.

Conclusion

Narcissism in the workplace can appear in many forms, from the coworker who takes all the praise to the boss who expects constant admiration. Over time, these habits wear down trust, harm group projects, and prompt valued employees to leave. Yet, companies and individuals are not powerless. Through strong HR practices, clear communication, and a culture that values shared success, workplaces can address these challenges.

On a personal level, employees can document issues, set boundaries, seek allies, and consider leaving if the environment remains toxic. Those who see narcissistic tendencies in themselves can choose to step back, listen more, and strive for genuine teamwork. The workplace, after all, is a shared space. By recognizing the signs of self-obsessed behavior and knowing how to respond, people can protect their professional growth and keep their tasks moving forward in a healthier, more respectful way.

In the chapters ahead, we will explore how technology and social media have become stages for self-obsessed behavior, the fine line between healthy confidence and narcissism, and more. Each setting reveals new angles on how people with these traits shape the world around them—and how others can respond effectively.

CHAPTER 11: NARCISSISM IN TECHNOLOGY AND SOCIAL MEDIA

Technology has changed how people connect with each other. Today, many of us carry devices that let us post our thoughts, pictures, and videos within seconds. This can be a great way to stay in touch, learn new things, and find support from friends near and far. But it can also become a stage for self-focused behavior. In this chapter, we will look at how technology and social media can encourage narcissistic habits, how online platforms can turn into places of constant self-promotion, and what steps we can take to avoid the traps of excessive self-obsession.

The Rise of Self-Display

One of the biggest changes in the online age is the ease of sharing personal moments. Not long ago, people took pictures with a camera and might show them to close friends or family members. These days, it is common to post photos for many people—sometimes hundreds or thousands—to see. This can include selfies, videos of daily activities, or snapshots of fancy meals. While it can be fun to share, it also introduces new ways to seek approval.

Some people feel a rush when they get likes or comments on a post. That little burst of attention can be exciting. Over time, the desire to keep getting that attention might grow. A person might start posting more often or trying to make their images look more dramatic. They might use filters and editing apps to appear flawless. In extreme cases, every activity becomes a chance to gather praise: from traveling to working out to eating lunch.

It is not always wrong to post about one's life. Many folks do this as a casual way to connect with friends. The difference appears when someone spends large amounts of time staging their posts, staring at the comment count, and feeling upset if they do not get enough admiration. That is when normal sharing can slip into a self-obsessed mindset. They begin to see social media as a performance stage rather than a friendly space.

Influencer Culture

Social media has also given rise to a new form of fame: the online influencer. These are individuals who have large followings and can sway what others think or buy. Sometimes, influencers create content about makeup, fitness, cooking, or other topics that interest many viewers. They may receive money or gifts from brands eager to reach their fans. While some influencers focus on sharing real tips and insights, others might center their entire presence on showing off a perfect life. Their posts might make it seem like they always look great, travel first class, or eat in fancy restaurants.

This can create unrealistic standards. People who follow them might feel they are missing out. Some decide they want to become influencers themselves, posting content in hopes of gathering a large fan base. In certain situations, the line between healthy self-expression and vanity can blur. A user might fixate on growing their follower count or boosting their post engagement, treating each like a mark of self-worth.

For someone who already shows narcissistic traits, influencer culture can reinforce self-centered behavior. Every like or new follower can act like a little trophy, feeding a belief that they deserve admiration. They might see their fans as numbers rather than real people, paying little attention to how their posts affect viewers. They may also chase controversy or drama just to stay in the spotlight. Over time, their sense of identity might become tightly tied to their online image.

Filters, Editing, and Reality Distortion

Modern technology lets users edit or enhance images with ease. Filters can smooth skin, brighten colors, and reshape features until the picture no longer shows reality. Some apps even offer face-tuning that can drastically change how someone looks. While some edits are harmless—like removing red eye—others can push an image far from the truth.

This distortion can impact both the poster and the audience. The poster may come to believe they should always look like the edited version, feeling unhappy about their real appearance. They might worry that if people saw them without filters, they would lose approval. Meanwhile, viewers might see these images and think, "Why don't I look like that?" not realizing the picture is heavily edited.

In a world where self-worth is tied to appearance, these tools can feed a narcissistic view. A person could spend hours perfecting each photo, ignoring friends or responsibilities. They might post only images that show them in an unrealistically positive light. If they get enough likes, they might feel a short boost, but it is not real confidence—it is tied to a fake image. This can lead to a cycle of chasing digital praise without any deeper sense of self-awareness.

Online Validation and Its Impact

One reason social media can encourage self-obsession is the constant feedback loop. Each post often receives immediate responses—thumbs up, hearts, or comments. For people with narcissistic leanings, this feedback can be addictive. They may check their phones many times a day to see if new notifications have appeared. If the reaction is strong, they feel proud. If it is weak, they may feel annoyed or depressed, blaming followers for "not appreciating them."

This pattern can change how a person behaves offline as well. They might choose their actions based on how share-worthy they are. For instance, instead of genuinely enjoying a concert, they might stand at the best angle to record a video for social media. They might pick travel spots mainly for the photo opportunities. Over time, life becomes a series of potential posts rather than real experiences.

In some cases, the search for online validation can also breed envy. Users might compare their engagement with others, feeling they are in a race to gather more praise. This can spark competitiveness or even push some to purchase fake likes or followers. These acts often create a false image that hides deeper insecurities. While it might look like success from the outside, it offers little real satisfaction and can crumble if exposed.

Cyberbullying and Harassment

Though it might seem that a self-focused person would not waste time on attacks, narcissistic traits can lead to hostile acts online. Some might belittle others to keep themselves on top. They could post mean comments, target specific users, or spread rumors. When confronted, they might insist they were only joking or say the victim is too sensitive. This behavior can cause serious harm to others, leading to anxiety, sadness, or fear of going online.

In some cases, the narcissistic individual sees bullying as a way to stay in control. By knocking someone else down, they feel bigger. They might rally a few followers to join them in mocking a target. This can create a stressful environment for anyone who crosses their path. The platform may have rules against bullying, but not all sites enforce them strongly. As a result, the narcissistic bully can continue for a long time without consequences, unless people speak up or the site administrators take action.

Chasing Viral Moments

Another factor is the allure of going viral. Many people share memes, funny videos, or shocking clips that spread quickly across the internet. Going viral can bring short bursts of fame, turning an unknown user into an overnight sensation. For someone already leaning toward self-focus, the quest to go viral can become a major goal. They might create stunts or controversies just to gain clicks and attention.

While a viral moment can feel exciting, it often fades fast. The internet moves on, looking for the next big thing. If a user becomes addicted to that kind of intense attention, they might keep pushing boundaries, becoming more extreme in their behavior or content. This can lead them to ignore ethics, relationships, and even safety. All that matters is that next wave of digital applause, no matter who gets hurt or misled in the process.

Gaming Platforms and Online Forums

It is not just social media sites that can feed narcissism; online gaming and forums can also create spaces for self-obsessed acts. In gaming, a narcissistic player might boast nonstop about their rank or their wins, belittling teammates for not performing as well. They might rage when they lose, blaming everyone else. These acts can spoil the fun for others who just want to play and cooperate.

On forums or community boards, a self-focused person might hijack discussions, turn topics into self-praise, or refuse to accept other opinions. They may argue tirelessly, feeling any challenge to their view is a personal attack. This can discourage others from sharing, turning what should be open conversation into a one-person show. Over time, the forum might lose its sense of community.

The Mask of Anonymity

Online anonymity can give people freedom to share personal thoughts they might hide in real life. However, it can also give narcissistic users a chance to act in ways they would not dare face-to-face. They might post extreme content, write hateful comments, or pretend to be experts on every subject. In some cases, they might create multiple accounts to boost their own posts, giving off a fake sense of widespread support.

This hiding behind a screen can reinforce self-obsession because there is little accountability. If a user offends someone, they can vanish or switch to a different username. They may not see the real harm they cause, viewing their online targets as faceless strangers. Over time, this can lead them deeper into a habit of using the internet for personal gain, ignoring the effects on others.

Parental Guidance and Young Users

Children and teens are growing up in a world where social media is the norm. Many start using platforms or gaming sites from a young age. While this can build digital skills, it can also place them in contact with narcissistic influences before they have the life experience to handle it.

A young person might learn that posting selfies with the right filter or showing certain behaviors gets them the most praise. Over time, they could shape their identity around seeking digital approval. If parents are not aware, the child could grow up believing that worth is measured by likes or comments. They may also encounter online bullying by self-obsessed peers who put others down to appear important.

Parents can help by having open talks about what it means to post something, how editing tools change images, and why empathy matters. Teaching them to think about how their posts affect others can build a healthier approach. This may not block all risks, but it can give children a stronger sense of perspective.

Setting Boundaries on Technology Use

For anyone struggling with self-focused online habits, setting limits can make a difference. This might include scheduling times to be offline or turning off social media notifications so they do not become a constant distraction. Some people find it helpful to keep their phones in another room at bedtime, preventing late-night scrolling or the temptation to check for new engagement.

Another idea is to set personal goals for online interactions, such as commenting supportively on friends' posts rather than competing for attention. This shift in mindset can change social media from a stage for self-promotion to a place of real exchange. Of course, these choices require self-awareness and a desire to change. If a person does not see a problem, they are not likely to limit their online habits.

Authenticity and Digital Minimalism

Digital minimalism refers to using technology in ways that serve genuine needs rather than letting apps or devices drive our choices. For someone trying to avoid self-obsession, this can be very helpful. They might decide to post only content that feels real and meaningful, not just what might get the most attention. They could reduce the number of platforms they use, focusing on smaller circles of real friends instead of chasing huge followings.

Authenticity also helps. When someone shares a real thought or feeling—warts and all—it can bring deeper connections than a polished image. They may feel less stressed about maintaining a flawless persona. Instead, they can focus on sharing honest experiences. This can open the door to support from true friends and help them break out of the cycle of seeking empty praise.

Tech Platforms and Responsibility

Some people argue that the designs of popular social media platforms encourage self-centered behavior. Features like "like counters," popularity rankings, or trending hashtags can push users to chase big numbers. In response, some platforms have tested hiding like counts or giving users more control over what they see. These small changes may help curb vanity metrics, but they do not solve the issue alone.

Platforms could also do more to curb harassment or bullying. Clear rules, fast reporting tools, and fair enforcement can reduce the chance that narcissistic users run rampant. However, the global nature of the internet makes this tough. Each country or region might have different laws. Some sites might prioritize profits and traffic over a healthy culture. For now, the burden often falls on users to set their own boundaries, block or report harmful accounts, and seek positive ways to engage online.

Protecting One's Self-Worth Offline

Because narcissistic behavior thrives on external applause, building self-worth offline can help protect against it. A person who feels good about their skills, friendships, and values in the real world is less likely to chase endless praise online. They can still enjoy sharing updates, but they will not be as shaken if the internet fails to adore them one day.

This might involve finding hobbies that do not rely on an audience—like painting for personal joy or learning a new skill quietly. It could also mean spending more time with friends in face-to-face gatherings, having real talks, or taking walks outside without feeling the need to share every step.

When we place more value on real-world experiences and personal growth, we are less tempted by the hollow form of approval that likes and follows provide. This does not mean quitting social media altogether. Instead, it means viewing online platforms as tools rather than as the center of our identity.

Warning Signs and Self-Check

If you notice that you or someone close to you is drifting into self-obsessed online behavior, some signs might include:

- **Frequent Mood Swings Based on Engagement:** Feeling very high or very low depending on how many likes or positive comments a post receives.
- **Editing or Filtering Every Post:** Never being satisfied with a normal picture, always feeling the need to enhance or reshape it.
- **Neglecting Offline Life:** Missing out on real social events or chores because of the urge to stay online or plan the next post.
- **Obsessing Over Follower Counts:** Checking stats many times a day, comparing them with others, and feeling threatened if a friend's profile grows faster.
- **Bullying or Stalking Others:** Sending harmful messages, making rude comments, or following someone around online for the thrill of control or to spark drama.
- **Taking Risks for Content:** Doing dangerous stunts or violating privacy just to capture attention online.

Not everyone who shows a few of these behaviors is a lost cause. Sometimes, people realize what they are doing and adjust their habits. Others might need a friend to gently say, "You've been spending a lot of time chasing approval. Is everything okay?" In more severe cases, talking with a counselor can help uncover what is fueling the need for constant recognition and how to build healthier self-esteem.

Conclusion

Technology and social media have made it easy for us to share our lives, learn from others, and stay connected. But these same tools can also spark or worsen narcissistic habits if we let them become the main source of approval. People may get caught in cycles of posting perfect images, seeking endless likes, or creating drama to remain relevant. Over time, this can drain them of genuine satisfaction and isolate them from real human bonds.

None of this means we must abandon devices or apps. The key is awareness and balance. By setting healthy boundaries, seeking real connections, and focusing on offline growth, we can enjoy the good aspects of online life without sliding into self-obsession. Platforms can also do their part by designing features that value thoughtful interaction over raw popularity numbers. In the end, technology is only a tool. How we use it—whether for learning, genuine sharing, or empty self-promotion—is up to each of us.

Next, we will explore the thin line that divides healthy self-confidence from harmful narcissism. While they can appear similar on the surface, their roots and outcomes are quite different. Understanding how to tell them apart can help us support healthy self-worth while avoiding the pitfalls of self-centered thinking.

CHAPTER 12: THE THIN LINE BETWEEN CONFIDENCE AND NARCISSISM

Confidence is often viewed as a good trait. It helps people apply for new jobs, speak up for themselves, and take on challenges. Someone who believes in their abilities can reach goals and bounce back from setbacks. However, sometimes it can be tricky to tell if a person is simply sure of themselves or drifting toward a self-obsessed style. In this chapter, we will look at what sets healthy confidence apart from narcissism, why that line can be confusing, and ways to support genuine self-respect without sliding into harmful self-importance.

What Is Healthy Confidence?

Healthy confidence involves a balanced view of one's skills and worth. A confident person recognizes they can do certain things well, but they also see that everyone has flaws or limits. They do not need nonstop praise to feel okay, and they can handle defeats or criticism without seeing them as personal attacks. In fact, a confident person might welcome feedback, viewing it as a tool for improvement.

When someone is truly confident, they do not feel threatened by the success of others. Instead, they can offer praise or show encouragement. They understand that another person's achievement does not take away from their own. In friendships, they are often supportive listeners, offering help or tips if asked. At work, they contribute ideas without pushing others aside. Overall, their sense of value feels steady, not easily shaken by day-to-day ups and downs.

How Narcissism Differs

In contrast, a narcissistic person tends to exaggerate their importance. They might see themselves as more talented or worthy than the rest, demanding that others treat them as superior. If they face criticism or failure, they might lash out or blame outside factors. This reaction stems from an inner fragility—the opposite of the genuine security that comes with real confidence.

Also, unlike the confident person who can share the spotlight, a narcissistic individual fights to remain in the center. They might interrupt or dismiss what others say. They may take credit for group successes. Their focus on their own image is so strong that they have less empathy for others. Success in the group setting is less about teamwork and more about personal glory.

Overlapping Traits and Confusion

Even though confidence and narcissism differ in core ways, they can look similar from the outside. Both a confident and a narcissistic person may appear proud of their accomplishments, speak with assurance, and stand up for themselves. Their peers may see them as strong or determined. So how can we tell them apart?

1. **Response to Criticism:** A confident person might ask for more details when criticized, aiming to learn. A narcissist might respond with anger, denial, or insults.
2. **Team Play:** A confident person shows respect for others' roles and ideas. A narcissist tries to dominate, ignoring or belittling suggestions from others.
3. **Expressions of Pride vs. Bragging:** A confident person might state a fact about an achievement, but they do not boast nonstop. A narcissist tends to keep the focus on personal glory, repeating the same stories of success again and again.
4. **Handling Other People's Success:** A confident person can feel happy for a friend's win. A narcissist may feel threatened or jealous, seeing it as a loss for themselves.
5. **Empathy:** Confidence does not rule out caring. Narcissism often does. A self-centered individual rarely steps into another person's shoes.

While none of these signs alone is a perfect measure, looking at the overall pattern can help. If you see consistent behaviors like anger at mild critique, constant bragging, or jealousy when others do well, those are clues the behavior is not just confidence.

Roots of Genuine Self-Esteem

Real self-esteem often develops from facing challenges, learning from mistakes, and seeing one's improvement over time. For example, a student who struggles with math might practice hard and improve their grades. They gain pride from knowing the work paid off. This sense of earned success tends to be stable; it does not vanish if they later get a low score. Instead, they see the setback as part of the learning process.

Other experiences that boost true self-esteem include:

- **Receiving Constructive Feedback:** Mentors or teachers who point out both strengths and areas to work on help a learner grow. They show that it is okay not to be perfect.
- **Developing Personal Values:** When a person knows their moral standards—like honesty or kindness—they can feel good about themselves for living by them, not just for external achievements.
- **Contributing to Others:** Volunteering time or helping friends can increase a sense of worth. Rather than grabbing praise for a solo act, the person sees the good they do in a wider group.
- **Testing Themselves Over Time:** Trying new tasks, failing at some, and gradually getting better can build confidence. This type of growth is grounded in real effort, not wishful thinking.

These methods help form a steady sense of self. That way, even if people criticize or life throws obstacles in the way, the foundation does not crumble.

How Narcissistic Self-View Takes Shape

In contrast, a narcissistic style can arise from shaky self-worth. Sometimes, a child grows up with extreme praise or is told they are flawless. They learn to expect constant admiration. Or they might have had the opposite, facing harsh rejection or feeling unseen, which leads them to develop a false front of superiority as self-protection.

As they move through life, they look for new ways to feel special. They might boast, fish for compliments, or try to prove they are better than others. If they do not receive the admiration they crave, they can react strongly because it pokes at an inner fear of not being good enough. This is different from genuine confidence, which stays steady even without applause.

Common Misconceptions

Many people assume that narcissists are simply people who have "too much self-love." But in reality, the narcissistic person's self-admiration is often fragile, built on external praise rather than deep acceptance of who they are. They might act bold on the outside but can feel insecure inside.

Another misconception is that confident people never doubt themselves. This is not true. A confident person may still wonder if they chose the best path or if they need more practice. The difference is that they do not crumble under doubt. They are open to learning and improving.

Signs of Balanced Self-Assurance

It can help to know what healthy, balanced self-assurance looks like in daily life. Such a person:

- **Values Others' Thoughts:** They listen when someone speaks and ask questions. They do not feel every idea they have is automatically best.
- **Can Laugh at Themselves:** They do not mind gentle teasing or pointing out minor flaws. They recognize that nobody is perfect.
- **Gives and Receives Compliments Well:** They show genuine joy when others do well and can accept praise without fishing for more. They also do not shrug off compliments; they can say "Thank you" and move on.
- **Admits Mistakes:** They handle errors by addressing what went wrong and trying to fix it. They do not try to cover up or shift blame just to protect an image.
- **Takes Care of Others' Needs:** While they stand up for themselves, they also understand the importance of teamwork and mutual respect.

Helping Someone Struggling with Narcissistic Traits

If you suspect a friend or family member is sliding from confidence into self-obsession, there might be ways to guide them toward a healthier mindset. It is not always simple, as people with self-centered habits can be defensive or angry when confronted. Still, gentle steps can have an effect:

1. **Encourage Honest Self-Reflection:** Suggest talking with a counselor or reading about emotional growth. If they see reliable sources describing narcissism, they might connect some dots.
2. **Avoid Constant Flattery:** If you keep boosting a narcissistic person's inflated view, you reinforce their need for it. That does not mean you must withhold all praise, but try to keep it genuine and balanced. If they do well, acknowledge it; if they are rude or hurtful, do not excuse it.
3. **Model Humility and Empathy:** Show by example how to accept feedback, admit mistakes, and appreciate others. When they see that you can be confident while still valuing different views, it might encourage them to rethink their own stance.
4. **Set Boundaries:** If they are always dominating conversations, kindly point out that you would like a turn to share your thoughts. If they belittle others, calmly say you do not support such behavior. Over time, they might learn that their self-obsessed ways push people away.

Building or Rebuilding Real Confidence

For those who find themselves unsure if their self-esteem is genuine or inflated, there are ways to build or rebuild honest self-confidence:

- **Seek Feedback from Trusted People:** Talk with a supportive friend, mentor, or therapist. Ask how you come across in group settings. Are you a good listener? Are you too quick to boast? That input can be eye-opening.
- **Keep a Realistic Record of Growth:** Write down your successes and areas you can improve. Reflect on what helped you succeed, whether it was practice, teamwork, or luck. Seeing the bigger picture keeps you grounded.

- **Face Failures with Openness:** If something goes wrong, try to see it as a learning moment, not a final verdict. Ask yourself what went wrong and how to do better next time.
- **Focus on Process, Not Just Results:** Whether you are writing a book, learning an instrument, or building a business, try to enjoy the steps involved. Confidence grows when you see that you can handle each part of the task, not only the end goal.
- **Give Back:** Spend time helping others with no thought of reward. This might be volunteering, mentoring someone, or simply being a supportive friend. It strengthens a sense of worth that does not rely on being the star of the show.

When Confidence Helps, and When It Harms

Healthy confidence can push people to try new activities, accept leadership roles, or stand up against unfairness. It can inspire others to do the same. A person who feels secure might mentor coworkers or share knowledge freely. In these ways, confidence adds to a group rather than taking from it.

Narcissism, however, often leads to broken trust, arguments, and frustration. Instead of encouraging others, a self-obsessed person sees them as rivals or tools. This can create a toxic environment at work or in a friend circle. While the narcissistic person might feel powerful in the short term, it can block them from building long-term relationships that provide real support and warmth.

Spotting Narcissism in Everyday Interactions

You might meet someone at an event who seems very sure of themselves. They talk about their projects with passion and appear ready to tackle big tasks. But do they ever pause to hear your input? Do they push aside your experiences or treat them like they do not matter?

If you notice that the person never asks about you, never listens, or becomes annoyed if you share a success story, they might not be just confident. They may be leaning toward a self-focused view of the world. This does not mean you must cut them off right away, but understanding the difference can help you manage your expectations. You might keep your topics light or limit your time around them if they do not show mutual respect.

Balancing Self-Confidence in Social Media

As covered in the previous chapter, technology can feed self-centered thinking. Yet it can also showcase honest confidence. If you are proud of a personal achievement—like finishing a tough project—you might post about it to share good news. That is normal. The key is how you respond to others and how you handle the feedback. If you keep the post real and remain open to conversation, you are likely in the zone of healthy confidence. If you obsess over how many likes you get or snap at anyone who does not praise you, you might be veering off track.

Teaching Young People the Difference

Adults who guide children or teens can help them tell apart confidence from self-focus. For instance, if a teen does well in a school play, it is good to say, "You put in so much effort, and your performance showed real skill!" That highlights the teen's work, not just the end result. If the teen then brags nonstop or looks down on classmates who also practiced hard, the adult might remind them that each cast member played a part. This helps the teen see that being proud of their role does not mean ignoring others' efforts.

Likewise, teaching empathy at a young age helps children understand the value of lifting up others. They learn that praising a friend's success does not reduce their own sense of worth. Over time, these lessons can shape a balanced view of self and others, preventing the growth of self-obsessed habits.

Reflections for Ourselves

We all have days when we feel pleased with our abilities and days when we feel uncertain. That is natural. The line between confidence and narcissism is crossed when we begin to see ourselves as more important than other people's feelings or contributions, or when we cannot handle even small criticisms without lashing out.

A good self-check is to notice how often you talk about your own successes compared to how often you show interest in others. Also, consider how you act when you fail or get negative feedback. Do you see it as a chance to learn, or do you get angry and shift blame? If you find that your behavior leans toward the latter, it might be time to practice more humility, ask for honest input, and remember that growth often comes from hearing what we can improve.

Conclusion

Confidence and narcissism might look alike on the surface—both involve a belief in one's abilities. However, they stand apart in key ways. True confidence rests on a steady sense of worth and welcomes growth, while narcissism relies on external praise and rejects anything that challenges a carefully built image. Confident individuals do not need to tear others down to feel secure, whereas self-obsessed folks often do. Understanding these distinctions helps us support healthy self-esteem in ourselves and those around us.

By valuing respect, empathy, and honest reflection, we can build a kind of confidence that stands strong, even when life gets hard. This approach goes beyond showy displays or the need to be on top. It focuses on personal growth, genuine connections, and a sense of self that does not crumble under setbacks. Keeping this perspective in mind helps us avoid slipping into harmful self-focus. In the chapters to come, we will continue exploring myths about narcissism, how it ties to self-esteem, and how to handle harmful behavior when it shows up in our personal or professional lives.

CHAPTER 13: MYTHS AND MISCONCEPTIONS

When people talk about narcissism, various beliefs and ideas often come up. Some might say, "All narcissists love themselves and show it constantly." Others might claim, "They are hopeless; no one with narcissistic behavior can change." Many of these statements are either oversimplifications or misunderstandings about what narcissism really is and how it shows up in everyday life. In this chapter, we will examine some common myths and misconceptions that surround self-obsessed behavior. By clearing up these misunderstandings, we can develop a more accurate view of what narcissism involves, how it grows, and what might be done about it.

Myth 1: Narcissists Always Have High Self-Esteem

A very frequent misconception is that a self-obsessed individual feels amazing about who they are. The belief is that they walk around with huge confidence and do not care about anything else. In truth, many narcissistic people are not as self-assured as they look. Their outward display of superiority often hides deeper worries or a shaky sense of worth. They might appear bold or unstoppable, but inside, they can be haunted by the fear that they are not as impressive as they claim to be.

Why This Matters

This hidden fragility helps explain why a person with narcissistic traits can overreact to even small criticisms. Their self-esteem might be like a balloon filled with too much air—any little poke feels like a threat that could pop it. Because of this, they might lash out, blame others, or try to shift attention somewhere else. Understanding that some narcissistic people have deeper insecurities can help us see why they behave the way they do.

Myth 2: Narcissistic Behavior Is Always Obvious

Some people think of a narcissist as someone who never stops bragging. While that can be true in some cases, there are also individuals who show self-obsession in more subtle ways. They might not boast openly, but they still focus a lot on themselves. This can come out as constantly steering conversations to their own interests, expecting special favors, or becoming upset if they are not given priority.

Hidden Forms

Some narcissistic individuals can even appear shy at times. This is sometimes referred to as "vulnerable narcissism." They might present themselves as sensitive or worried about what people think, yet they still expect others to treat them as special. If they feel ignored, they could become tearful or upset in a way that pulls attention back to them. The key point is that not every self-obsessed person is loud. Some may act timid on the surface, but their actions still revolve around a need for special treatment.

Myth 3: Narcissism Is the Same as Being Confident

People often confuse a healthy sense of confidence with narcissism. In earlier chapters, we touched on the differences. True confidence is built on a balanced view of one's strengths and weaknesses. A confident individual can admit mistakes, listen to others, and does not feel threatened by someone else's success.

Where the Confusion Comes From

A narcissistic person and a confident person might both display pride in what they do well. However, the narcissist's pride often requires them to look down on others. If they cannot place themselves above someone, they may feel uneasy or offended. Meanwhile, a genuinely confident person can shine without putting anyone else down. By looking at how someone handles feedback, shares space, and respects other people's talents, we can tell real confidence from a self-centered outlook.

Myth 4: Narcissism Is Always a Choice

Some think narcissistic behavior is a deliberate decision that can simply be turned off if the individual wants to. But self-obsession often grows from complex factors like upbringing, personal traits, early experiences of being over-praised or severely criticized, and possibly deeper emotional problems. Many people with narcissistic habits might not fully realize how their behavior affects others.

The Role of Awareness

This does not excuse harmful actions, but it suggests that breaking self-focused patterns can be harder than just "waking up one morning and stopping." It can involve unlearning deep-rooted views and coping methods. Therapy or counseling often helps people see how their mind works, where their fears come from, and what steps can be taken to form healthier habits. Telling a narcissistic person "Stop being selfish" usually does little unless they are ready to examine why they became that way in the first place.

Myth 5: Narcissists Never Help Others

Another misconception is that people with narcissistic traits never do anything for anyone else. In reality, some can be quite helpful or generous when it suits them, especially if it boosts their image. For instance, a narcissistic individual may donate to a charity and then make sure everyone knows about it. Or they might do someone a favor but remind the person repeatedly that they owe them for the favor.

Doing Good Deeds for Applause

The main difference is that their helping behavior is often linked to a desire for praise or a return favor, rather than pure kindness. If they sense that helping will elevate their status or earn public admiration, they might jump in eagerly. However, if no one is watching or if they get no direct benefit, they might not be motivated to give their time or resources. This does not mean every act of kindness is fake, but it highlights that the drive for praise often plays a strong role.

Myth 6: Narcissism Only Affects People Around Middle Age

Some believe that self-obsession primarily appears in adulthood, maybe after certain life successes or setbacks. However, as covered in earlier chapters, signs of self-focused behavior can surface in childhood or teenage years. A person does not have to wait until they are middle-aged to show traits like needing constant praise, manipulating others, or struggling with criticism.

Different Life Stages

Narcissistic traits can also shift as someone grows older. A child might show it by refusing to share toys and throwing big tantrums if not praised. A teenager might expect special treatment at school or brag ceaselessly online. An adult might sabotage coworkers to get ahead. While the outside behavior looks different, the underlying pattern of self-centered thinking remains. This is why awareness at any age is important to prevent these traits from becoming stronger over time.

Myth 7: Narcissists Are Always the Life of the Party

Some people with narcissistic styles do love being the center of attention at social events. They might tell stories or jokes for a crowd, talking over others. But there are also narcissistic individuals who do not enjoy crowds at all. They might prefer one-on-one interactions where they can control the conversation or manipulate the other person more easily.

Quiet Manipulation

A person might be socially withdrawn yet still place themselves at the center of their own world. For instance, they could keep a small circle of acquaintances who validate their views. They might build an online presence where they can post selectively. The absence of party behavior does not guarantee someone is not self-obsessed. Narcissism is about an inflated sense of self-worth and the actions that arise from it, not necessarily about being outgoing or shy.

Myth 8: They Are Incapable of Feeling Sadness or Worry

It is false to think that people with narcissistic traits never feel negative emotions like sadness, worry, or regret. In fact, some might experience these feelings deeply, especially if something threatens their idealized image of themselves. For example, losing a job or failing at a goal can send them into a spiral of anger and despair. They might blame others or feel the world is unfair to them.

Emotional Response

These individuals can experience a range of emotions but might handle them poorly. For instance, they might express sadness through anger or try to find someone else to blame for their disappointment. They might not show empathy when others suffer, but they can still feel pain for themselves. The difference is that they often filter these feelings through a lens of "How does this affect me?" rather than focusing on the shared experiences of humanity.

Myth 9: Everyone Has Some Narcissism, So It's Not a Real Problem

It is common for people to argue, "We all have moments of self-focus, so narcissism is just part of being human." While it is true that many people have small self-centered habits—like bragging occasionally or wishing for special treatment from time to time—that does not mean full-blown narcissism is universal or harmless.

The Difference Between Habit and Pattern

Normal self-focus in small doses is different from an ongoing pattern that causes harm. A person who occasionally boasts is not necessarily a narcissist. The concern arises when self-obsessed thinking dominates relationships, work life, and personal growth. That is when it becomes a serious issue, damaging the person's connections and well-being. Recognizing that difference helps us avoid dismissing narcissism as "something everyone does."

Myth 10: Narcissists Cannot Be Intelligent or Successful

Some might think that people with self-obsessed traits are bound to fail in life. They may believe that because narcissistic folks have trouble getting along with others, they cannot hold jobs or be high achievers. This overlooks the fact that certain narcissistic traits—like boldness, willingness to take risks, or capacity to promote oneself—can lead to tangible success in certain fields.

Possible Success but Risky Outcomes

A self-centered person might climb the ranks in a competitive work setting by pushing their own achievements and ignoring others. They could become leaders by appearing very sure of themselves. However, their success can be shaky if they burn too many bridges or ignore the concerns of others. Some hold high-level positions for a while but face crises when coworkers unite against them or when a scandal reveals their harmful behavior. So, while they can be very skilled or bright, they often leave behind a trail of unhappy colleagues or broken relationships.

Myth 11: They Do Not Need or Want Genuine Connections

It can seem like a self-obsessed person does not care about forming real bonds because they seem so wrapped up in themselves. However, many do crave connection. The problem is that their view of how relationships work may be skewed. They may seek relationships primarily to feel admired or validated. When those connections demand empathy and give-and-take, a narcissistic person can become frustrated, not understanding why their partner or friend wants attention too.

Craving but Struggling

In fact, some of them can feel lonely because they cannot maintain the close bonds they desire. Their actions sabotage the relationships they want. But simply wanting friends or a romantic partner does not erase the need for them to learn healthier ways to relate. This means that while they may claim to want love and closeness, the patterns they use often get in the way, leading to repeated problems.

Myth 12: Only Men Can Be Narcissistic

A long-standing stereotype suggests that men are more likely to be self-obsessed, possibly due to cultural roles or expectations about assertiveness. While research shows certain forms of narcissistic personality style can be more common in men, many women can also develop these traits. The difference might be in how it shows up, shaped by social expectations.

Gender and Presentation

Some women with narcissistic tendencies might place heavy focus on appearance or social status. Others might show controlling behavior within a family setting. The core trait—an inflated sense of self-importance—can appear in any gender. Assuming it is exclusive to men can cause people to miss signs of harmful behavior in women or others.

Myth 13: Narcissism Is Never Mixed with Other Issues

Another misconception is that narcissism exists in a bubble. In reality, a self-obsessed style can overlap with other mental or behavioral challenges. For example, a person might struggle with anxiety or depression, using a narcissistic front to cope. They might also deal with addictive behaviors, trying to mask feelings of emptiness. Sometimes, the lines blur, making it tricky to see where one issue ends and another begins.

A Complex Picture

If a person seeks professional help, the therapist might discover layers of problems. Treating only one aspect (for example, telling them to stop bragging) may not help if there are deeper roots of trauma or insecurity. That is why a thorough approach is needed, looking at emotional history, thought patterns, and present life context.

Myth 14: You Can Fix a Narcissist by Appeasing Them

Some people think, "If I just give them the praise they want, we'll have peace." Though this might calm a situation briefly, constantly feeding someone's need for admiration does not solve the underlying patterns. It can even enable them to keep acting in destructive ways. Over time, the person with narcissistic traits may only demand more. This can drain the emotional reserves of the people around them and keep everyone stuck.

Real Change vs. Temporary Peace

Real improvement requires the individual to see how their behavior affects others and to learn new skills, such as healthy self-soothing, empathy, and emotional regulation. Family members or friends who keep giving in to them out of fear or exhaustion might only be postponing bigger conflicts. The person never gets the message that their behavior is problematic if everyone tiptoes around them.

Myth 15: Narcissistic Traits Cannot Decrease with Age

Some assume that once self-focused habits form, they are set in stone. Yet, like many personality patterns, narcissism can shift over the years. Older adults might soften if they face losses or discover that their old ways of relating do not hold up. Some might become more reflective and humble as they age. However, others might dig in further, especially if they cling to old coping methods.

Openness to Growth

Whether narcissistic traits lessen may depend on whether the person faces consequences and becomes open to self-awareness. Age alone does not guarantee change. If someone keeps receiving what they want or stays in denial, their behavior might stay the same. But if life events force them to rethink, there can be room for adjustment, just as with other patterns.

How Myths Block Understanding

Believing these myths can cause several problems. First, it can lead us to see self-obsessed people as one-dimensional, missing the varied ways narcissism appears. Second, myths can make it harder to respond effectively. For instance, if we think that only men can be narcissistic, we might fail to notice signs in a female friend or family member. If we believe that narcissists are always proud and fearless, we might not recognize that some actually struggle with deep insecurities.

Bustling these myths helps us spot narcissism more accurately. We see that it can show up in many forms: loud, quiet, or somewhere in between. We learn that narcissistic traits are not always fueled by a genuine sense of self-worth, and that they can coexist with other mental or emotional challenges.

Steps to Counter These Misconceptions

1. **Look for Patterns, Not Just Moments:** Recognize that narcissism is about ongoing behavior. One act of bragging does not always mean a person is self-obsessed. Notice if there is a pattern of needing to be above others, ignoring boundaries, or reacting strongly to criticism.
2. **Acknowledge Many Faces of Self-Focus:** Remember that some individuals might appear shy or even helpful but still be driven by a need for constant admiration. Try to see how they act across different situations, not just in one setting.
3. **Seek Credible Information:** There are many resources—like reliable articles, books, and mental health professionals—that can share deeper insights on narcissism. Getting facts from experts can clear up any incorrect beliefs.
4. **Avoid Blanket Labels:** It helps to be careful when labeling someone as a narcissist right away. Instead, look at specific behaviors. Do they manipulate frequently? Do they turn every conversation to themselves? This detail-oriented view is more accurate than broad assumptions.
5. **Stay Open to Growth:** Remember that some individuals with narcissistic behavior can learn new ways of relating if they are willing. While it is not guaranteed, do not assume all hope is lost. At the same time, be realistic about the effort it takes to shift deep-rooted habits.

The Value of Understanding

When myths go unchecked, it is easy to misjudge people. We might think we are simply dealing with a rude coworker who loves themselves, when in fact they are deeply insecure and unable to handle honest feedback. Or we might fall for someone who acts sweet but uses subtle tactics to keep us focused on them. By breaking down these myths, we gain a clearer sense of when we are dealing with a real pattern of narcissistic behavior and what that entails.

This clarity is helpful for our own mental health. We avoid taking certain actions personally if we realize the other person's behavior stems from deeper issues. We can also decide better how to respond—whether by setting limits, seeking guidance from a professional, or stepping away if the connection is too harmful.

A Balanced Perspective

Narcissism is not about a single trait like bragging or being mean. It is a collection of beliefs and actions. Recognizing the myths and focusing on the truth helps us navigate the behaviors we see in ourselves or others. We can then move away from simple stereotypes and toward a more detailed, compassionate, but also realistic viewpoint.

- Some narcissistic people are loud and open; others are soft-spoken.
- They might come from various backgrounds or have different upbringings.
- They can be extremely good at certain tasks but struggle to keep stable relationships.
- They might both want and fear close bonds, creating confusing push-and-pull dynamics.

Having an informed viewpoint does not mean excusing bad behavior, but it can stop us from making overly broad judgments. It also helps us be better prepared if we choose to address these patterns—either in those around us or in ourselves.

Moving Forward

In the next chapter, we will address the difference between healthy self-esteem and narcissism in more detail. While we have touched on that contrast in many chapters, we will look specifically at how normal self-worth develops, how to keep it strong, and why narcissism can mislead a person into thinking they have self-esteem when they actually do not. Understanding these details can be a key step in supporting genuine personal growth and stopping the spread of harmful self-obsession.

For now, remember that myths often simplify complicated truths. By looking more closely, we see that narcissism can take many forms and arise from many sources. Not everyone with self-centered habits is doomed to remain that way forever. Yet, real change requires honest recognition of the problem and an interest in forming new patterns. Letting go of myths and seeing narcissism as it really is can open the door to more constructive approaches—both for ourselves and for the people we care about.

CHAPTER 14: SELF-ESTEEM VS. NARCISSISM

Self-esteem can give us a stable sense of who we are, guiding us through successes and challenges. Narcissism, however, often involves a shaky sense of self covered by a showy exterior. Though they might look alike from the outside—both can involve a person who speaks confidently or aims high—the differences are key to understanding which is healthy and which can lead to harm. In this chapter, we will explore how self-esteem grows, how narcissism mimics it but lacks its steady foundation, and ways to foster strong yet balanced self-worth.

Defining Self-Esteem

Self-esteem is the level of respect we hold for ourselves. It forms from the mix of experiences, feedback from others, personal beliefs, and lessons we learn. A person with healthy self-esteem generally feels worthy and capable, yet recognizes they are not perfect. They can handle challenges without feeling crushed when things go wrong.

Key features of healthy self-esteem:

- Comfort in one's own skin: Not feeling a need to constantly prove something.
- Openness to new tasks: Willingness to try, even if not guaranteed success.
- Acceptance of flaws: Understanding that everyone has weak spots or areas to improve.
- Ability to accept praise without craving it: Enjoying compliments but not relying on them as the sole measure of worth.

Where Does Self-Esteem Come From?

1. **Childhood Experiences:** Families that provide balance—offering love, encouragement, and guidance on improvement—help children develop a sense that they matter without feeling superior to everyone else.

2. **Learning and Growth:** School, sports, hobbies, and other activities teach a person about effort, success, and failure. Overcoming obstacles can build lasting confidence.
3. **Positive but Realistic Feedback:** Friends, teachers, and mentors who give honest praise and point out areas for growth can support a grounded sense of self.
4. **Personal Reflection:** As people grow older, they might examine what they care about—values, goals, and passions. Building life around these can help them feel stable and proud of who they are.
5. **Relationships and Community:** Feeling accepted among peers or in a group fosters a belief in one's value. This does not mean needing constant approval; rather, it is the sense of belonging that helps a person see they are not alone.

Over time, these factors shape a self-view that can remain strong without needing to be propped up by applause or superiority.

When Self-Esteem Becomes Fragile

Even a person with a fairly healthy sense of self can go through phases of doubt. Maybe they face a major setback like job loss or relationship troubles. This can shake their confidence for a bit. But if the foundation is solid, they will likely adjust and recover. However, if someone never formed genuine self-esteem, they might try to fill the gap by seeking praise, attention, or control over others.

This is where narcissism can creep in. When self-esteem is shaky, a person may develop a false front of being grand or special, hoping to hide their fears about not being good enough. That front might fool some observers for a while, but deep inside it does not feel stable. The person may crave more and more recognition, yet it never truly satisfies their underlying insecurity.

Comparing the Two: Self-Esteem vs. Narcissism

A handy way to see the difference is by looking at how each responds to everyday events:

1. **Dealing with Criticism**
   - Healthy Self-Esteem: "This feedback hurts a bit, but I can see how I can improve."
   - Narcissism: "How dare they question me? They must be jealous or out to get me."
2. **Interacting with Others' Success**
   - Healthy Self-Esteem: "It's great that my friend achieved that goal. I'm proud of them."
   - Narcissism: "Their success takes away from my spotlight. I should show why I'm better."
3. **Reacting to Failure**
   - Healthy Self-Esteem: "I made mistakes. I'll learn and do better next time."
   - Narcissism: "It wasn't my fault. Someone else must have messed up, or the rules were unfair."
4. **Source of Worth**
   - Healthy Self-Esteem: Balanced sense of self grounded in ability, values, and caring for others.
   - Narcissism: Strong need for external praise or visible achievements to feel okay.
5. **Empathy**
   - Healthy Self-Esteem: Understands that other people's feelings matter and can see situations from their viewpoint.
   - Narcissism: Struggles to imagine others' perspectives unless it directly affects personal image.

By focusing on these differences, we see that narcissism usually involves a stronger sense of threat whenever one's status or image is at stake.

Signs of True Self-Esteem

- **Calm Acceptance:** A person with genuine self-esteem does not need to be the best in every situation. They can step back and let others shine without feeling diminished.
- **Consistent Behavior:** They generally treat people with respect, whether it's a boss or a server at a cafe. Their sense of worth is not dependent on belittling anyone.

- **Honest Self-Talk:** When they do well, they can say, "I worked hard and did a good job." When they fail, they might say, "I have to try a different approach next time."
- **Balance of "Me" and "We":** They know their own strengths but also acknowledge the value of teamwork. They can work together without always needing to be in charge.

Why People Mistake Narcissism for Strong Self-Esteem

Sometimes, the loud, bold qualities of a narcissistic person can look like confidence. They might seem fearless and unstoppable. They speak about their goals in a grand way, and they might attract a following. People could admire them at first, thinking, "Here is someone who believes in themselves."

The difference becomes clear over time. True self-esteem does not require crushing others or ignoring their input. If someone constantly hogs credit and never shares the stage, that suggests an overreliance on external approval. We might see that they crumble in the face of even small failures, or that they cannot handle hearing anyone else praised. At that point, what looked like confidence starts to reveal itself as a fragile, self-centered style.

Problems That Arise When Narcissism Replaces Real Self-Esteem

When a person adopts narcissistic habits instead of building steady self-worth, problems usually follow:

1. **Shaky Relationships:** Friendships and romances can suffer because the narcissistic individual might not show consistent empathy or genuine care. They might act kindly if it wins them admiration, but let people down when there is no direct personal gain.
2. **Workplace Tensions:** Coworkers might resent someone who takes all the credit or blames others for every mistake. Teamwork can fall apart.
3. **Emotional Highs and Lows:** The narcissistic person may feel awesome when praised but sink into anger or gloom when challenged. This leads to mood swings and stress.

4. **Loneliness:** Over time, people might pull away from the narcissist. They do not want to be used or ridiculed. The self-obsessed individual might end up with few authentic bonds.
5. **Missed Growth Opportunities:** Because they cannot accept real feedback, the narcissistic person does not learn from errors. They may stay stuck in patterns that keep causing trouble.

Building or Rebuilding Healthy Self-Esteem

For someone who recognizes that they lack a stable sense of self, there are several steps to grow real self-esteem rather than masking insecurity with self-obsession:

1. **Self-Awareness:** Accept that your inner confidence might not be as solid as you want. This is often the hardest step because it can feel painful.
2. **Small Achievements:** Work on goals that matter to you, such as learning a new skill or completing a project. Celebrate (avoid that specific word—use "acknowledge" instead) the progress, not just the end result.
3. **Receiving Feedback Calmly:** Practice hearing input from others without snapping back. If you feel defensive, take a breath and remind yourself that feedback can help you improve.
4. **Sharing Praise:** Instead of trying to grab all admiration, look for ways to give credit to others. Over time, seeing others succeed alongside you can feel good.
5. **Seeking Professional Help:** A counselor or therapist can guide you in exploring the roots of low self-esteem and the reasons behind any self-obsessed defenses.
6. **Mindful Self-Talk:** Notice how you speak to yourself mentally. If you blame everyone else for problems or beat yourself up harshly, try to find balanced thoughts: "I made a mistake, but I can do better next time."

Parenting Approaches That Support Real Self-Esteem

For parents or guardians concerned about raising children with a healthy sense of self, there are constructive ways to encourage balanced confidence:

- **Offer Genuine Encouragement:** Point out specific things the child does well, but also be honest about areas for growth.
- **Model Humility:** Let children see that it is okay for you to make mistakes. Show how you handle setbacks calmly.
- **Avoid Over-Praising Everything:** Constantly telling a child they are the best can give them unrealistic views. Instead, praise actual effort or improvement.
- **Teach Empathy:** Encourage them to notice how others feel. Ask, "How do you think your friend felt when that happened?" This nurtures caring instead of self-focus.
- **Promote Sharing Credit:** In group activities, highlight the roles of all involved. This helps kids see that success is often a team effort.

The Role of Culture and Society

In some cultures or environments, people might be rewarded only when they appear to be the "top" individual. Social media often shines a light on those who boast the loudest or look the flashiest. Such settings might tempt a person to put on a narcissistic front even if they have a solid base of self-esteem, because big claims and showy posts get attention.

However, a culture that respects teamwork, empathy, and balanced self-image can help people develop real self-esteem. Schools and workplaces can teach skills like group discussion, fair play, and giving credit. Families can talk about the value of helping one another. All of this reduces pressure to appear perfect and encourages honest growth.

When Someone's Self-Esteem Is Unclear

Sometimes, we come across people who seem confident, but we cannot tell if it is real or not. Some questions to consider:

1. **Are they respectful of others?** Confidence often includes a respect for each person's dignity. If someone puts others down, it may be more self-obsession than real confidence.

2. **Do they handle setbacks maturely?** Look at how they respond when a plan fails or they receive a "no." True confidence can roll with the punches.
3. **Do they listen in conversations?** Healthy self-esteem leaves room for others to speak. A self-obsessed style might dominate discussions at all times.
4. **Is there a pattern of shifting blame?** A person with balanced self-esteem can own their part in mistakes. A narcissistic person tends to dodge accountability.

Supporting a Friend or Family Member

If you think someone you care about might lack a strong sense of self and is leaning toward self-obsessed behaviors, you can:

- **Offer Honest Yet Kind Feedback:** Gently point out moments when they disregard others or refuse to hear feedback. Show understanding but do not enable the behavior.
- **Encourage Self-Reflection:** Suggest they keep a journal or talk with a professional. Sometimes, writing down daily thoughts can reveal patterns they were unaware of.
- **Celebrate Meaningful Growth:** When they handle a challenge in a balanced way, acknowledge it. This might help them see the value of genuine self-esteem rather than chasing empty praise.
- **Set Boundaries:** If they constantly demand attention or admiration, calmly let them know it is not okay. This shows that relationships involve fairness and respect.

Pitfalls to Avoid

1. **Trying to "Fix" Them Alone:** If someone is deeply stuck in a self-obsessed style, one friend or family member cannot single-handedly solve it. They may need professional help.

2. **Praising Everything to Keep the Peace:** Showering them with flattery might patch things for a short time but does not address the real problem.
3. **Arguing Over Every Slight:** People with fragile self-worth can be easily provoked. While it is good to stand up for yourself, picking fights over every minor insult may worsen tensions.
4. **Neglecting Your Own Well-Being:** If you pour all your energy into someone else's self-esteem issues, you might ignore your own needs or goals. Keep an eye on your own mental and emotional health.

Final Thoughts on Self-Esteem vs. Narcissism

Healthy self-esteem is like a strong tree. It bends in the wind of life's challenges but stays rooted because its foundation is real. Narcissism is more like a tall mirror—reflective and attention-getting, but fragile. One push or crack can shatter the illusion of grandness. Recognizing the difference helps us build relationships and communities that value honesty, respect, and real personal growth.

- Self-esteem rests on genuine respect for oneself and others.
- Narcissism relies on external praise and often ignores others' needs.
- True confidence weathers setbacks; narcissism crumbles or blames.
- With awareness, people can move from shallow displays of grandeur to a steady, fulfilling sense of who they are.

In the chapters ahead, we will continue exploring the effects of narcissism on physical and emotional health and how to recognize when someone's behavior crosses a line into harm. This deeper look will underscore how vital it is to nurture real self-esteem—both for our own good and for the well-being of those around us.

CHAPTER 15: PHYSICAL AND EMOTIONAL CONSEQUENCES

When we think about self-obsessed behavior, we often focus on its effects on relationships or social settings. However, narcissistic traits can also influence a person's physical and emotional well-being in ways that might not be obvious at first. In this chapter, we will look at how a self-centered mindset can shape overall health, moods, stress levels, and even the body's response to challenges. We will also see how people close to a narcissistic individual may experience their own physical and emotional costs.

Stress and the Self-Obsessed Mindset

A person with strong self-focused traits can experience high levels of stress for a few reasons. First, they may have frequent conflicts with others. Arguing, blaming, or feeling offended all the time can keep the body and mind in a tense state. Such constant tension can increase the body's release of stress hormones like cortisol. Over time, high cortisol can contribute to problems with sleep, mood, and even the immune system.

Additionally, narcissistic individuals often feel great anxiety about appearing "perfect" in the eyes of those around them. They might worry a lot about whether people are giving them enough attention or admiration. This worry can lead to headaches, fatigue, or restlessness. Because self-obsessed people sometimes avoid learning from mistakes, they may repeat the same errors and face repeated stressful outcomes, such as job losses or ongoing family arguments.

Conflict on Many Fronts

Because of their need to be on top, narcissistic individuals might clash with bosses, colleagues, partners, friends, or family members. These disputes lead to an environment of constant tension. Even if they try to shift blame to others, the repeated arguments can still wear them down. A person may not admit they feel stressed, but their body might reflect it through high blood pressure, stomach problems, or trouble sleeping. In the long run, these signs can hint at deeper health concerns.

Emotional Ups and Downs

Although a self-obsessed individual can look confident and in control, their emotional state can be fragile. They might soar with excitement if someone praises them but crash if they are ignored or criticized. This pattern of highs and lows can strain the mind. Feeling one moment like a star and the next moment like a failure is exhausting. It can also confuse people around them, who never know what mood they will encounter.

The "Empty" Feeling

Some narcissistic individuals describe a lingering sense of emptiness, even though they try hard to gain admiration. They might receive attention but not feel truly satisfied. This can lead them to seek more praise, like a person drinking saltwater to quench thirst. No matter how much they get, it is never enough. This persistent emptiness can lead to sadness or frustration, as well as a sense of being misunderstood.

Anger and Resentment

Anger is also common. A self-obsessed person might feel insulted by small things, believing others are not giving them proper respect. If they lose out on a promotion or do not get first place in a contest, they might lash out, claiming unfairness. Over time, these angry moments can build up, affecting their emotional health. They may become bitter, blaming life for not granting them the status they believe they deserve. This bitterness can turn inward or outward, leading to further harm.

Physical Signs of Emotional Strain

Repeated emotional strain can show up in physical ways. Some of the more common examples include:

1. **Headaches or Migraines:** Continuous tension or anger can contribute to muscle tightness around the neck and shoulders.
2. **Stomach Issues:** Stress can lead to digestive problems such as heartburn, ulcers, or general stomach discomfort.
3. **High Blood Pressure:** Ongoing conflict and stress can push blood pressure up. Over time, this can put strain on the heart and blood vessels.
4. **Fatigue and Low Energy:** Being on guard all the time—trying to protect one's image—can sap energy levels. Some people may struggle to wake up or feel motivated.
5. **Sleep Problems:** Racing thoughts, worries about how others see them, or ongoing disagreements can keep a person awake at night. In turn, poor sleep worsens mood and stress levels during the day.

Not everyone will experience all these symptoms, but even a few can signal that something is out of balance. Over months or years, these health issues can grow more severe if no steps are taken to address the root causes.

Harm to Personal and Professional Growth

People who focus heavily on themselves might struggle to take care of their bodies in other ways. For instance, they might rely on quick fixes like fast food if they are too busy chasing praise to plan healthy meals. They may ignore routine medical checkups because they believe they are above normal concerns. Or they might skip exercise unless it directly feeds their image (for example, if it helps them look a certain way to get admiration, but not if it is for overall health).

Neglect of Genuine Self-Care

Real self-care involves tending to physical and emotional needs consistently—getting enough rest, eating nourishing foods, staying active in ways that help the mind and body. A self-obsessed person might talk about fitness if it wins them praise but ignore other important health routines. Over time, this can lead to chronic conditions or a weaker ability to fight illness.

Career Burnout

On the job, a self-obsessed individual may either push themselves too hard to stand out or sabotage relationships with coworkers. Both extremes carry risks.

Pushing too hard without collaboration can cause burnout. Alienating coworkers can lead to a hostile work setting, which adds to stress levels. Eventually, the combination of physical stress and poor social ties might lead to leaving a position or being forced out, creating more emotional turmoil.

Impact on Loved Ones

The people living with or close to a narcissistic individual can also face emotional and physical consequences. Constant arguments or manipulation can lead partners or family members to feel anxious or depressed. They might walk on eggshells, worried about triggering an outburst. This tension can disrupt their eating habits, sleep, or overall sense of peace.

Effects on Children

Children in a household with a narcissistic parent can develop chronic stress symptoms, such as stomach aches or headaches. They may struggle at school due to the emotional strain at home. They might also grow up thinking they must always please the self-focused parent, which can lead them to ignore their own needs. This can set them up for future difficulties in relationships and self-esteem.

Friends and Extended Family

Even friends or extended relatives can be pulled into drama. The narcissistic individual may call them to complain or brag, ignoring the friend's needs. Over time, this one-sided connection can wear the friend down, leading to lost friendships or repeated arguments. Meanwhile, if the friend tries to point out the problem, they might face anger, which adds to stress for both sides.

Emotional Exhaustion and "Burnout by Association"

Loved ones and friends of a self-obsessed person can experience what is sometimes called "burnout by association." This occurs when someone who is not narcissistic themselves feels drained or overwhelmed from constantly dealing with the self-focused individual's demands, mood swings, and conflicts. Symptoms may include:

- Feeling tired after every conversation or visit
- Anxiety about when the next crisis or conflict will occur
- Difficulty concentrating on personal tasks due to worry
- Trouble sleeping or frequent bad dreams about arguments
- Reduced self-confidence, particularly if they are repeatedly blamed for issues

If left unchecked, this type of secondary stress can harm a person's health. They may need to set firm boundaries, seek counseling, or limit contact for the sake of their own well-being.

Connection with Anxiety and Depression

A person with narcissistic traits might also show signs of anxiety or depression. At first, this might seem surprising, because they appear so proud or above it all. But deep within, a self-obsessed person can fear that their "perfect" mask will crack. They may fret about someone surpassing them or discovering their flaws. They could feel depressed when admiration is missing or if they face a major setback.

Masking Sadness with Anger

In some cases, sadness may present as anger or irritability. Instead of admitting they feel down, they lash out at those nearby. This can make it hard to recognize depression or address it in a helpful way. If they do get diagnosed with anxiety or depression, they might deny it or blame the doctor, claiming nobody understands them. This resistance to seeing themselves as less than perfect can delay proper treatment.

Risk-Taking and Health Hazards

Narcissistic individuals may also engage in risk-taking, believing they are too special for bad things to happen. This might include driving recklessly, spending large sums on credit, or ignoring health guidelines (for instance, skipping seat belts or refusing safe practices if they see them as a hassle). Such behaviors can lead to accidents or legal troubles.

If they do get hurt or face legal consequences, the self-obsessed person may deny responsibility, claiming they are a victim of bad luck or someone else's actions. Meanwhile, the physical and emotional cost can be significant—hospital stays, financial debt, and lingering mental stress.

Substance Use and Addiction

Sometimes, a self-centered individual might turn to alcohol or drugs, especially if they are feeling unhappy beneath the surface. They might say things like, "I can handle it" or "Rules do not apply to me." Over time, substance use can become a crutch to soothe their sense of emptiness or frustration when they are not receiving attention. Because they have trouble accepting faults, they could avoid admitting they have a problem.

Effect on Emotions and Relationships

Substance use can worsen mood swings, leading to more conflicts. It can also damage trust with loved ones. If someone is already on shaky ground due to narcissistic behavior, adding addiction can make the environment even more chaotic. Physical harm, legal problems, or long-lasting health damage can then follow, further adding to stress.

Self-Harm and Destructive Behaviors

Though it may sound contradictory, a small number of narcissistic individuals might engage in self-harm behaviors when they feel their grand image is threatened. They might reason that hurting themselves could force attention or pity from others. Or they might experience such intense self-hate during low moments that they lash out at their own bodies. This does not happen in all cases, but it can occur in those who have mixed emotional troubles beneath the self-centered mask.

If they do engage in self-harm, it often involves secrecy. They might be too proud to seek help openly or might expect others to notice without having to ask. This can create a dangerous situation in which the person avoids professional support because they want to keep up a front of strength.

The Role of Therapy and Support

Both narcissistic individuals and their loved ones can benefit from professional guidance in addressing physical and emotional consequences. Therapy might focus on:

1. **Stress Management:** Learning healthy ways to calm the mind and body, such as breathing techniques or light exercise.
2. **Emotional Awareness:** Helping the person notice when they feel anger, sadness, or fear, and teaching them to respond in healthier ways.
3. **Communication Skills:** Guiding them to speak and listen without dominating or blaming, improving relationships with partners, friends, and coworkers.
4. **Self-Care Routines:** Encouraging regular sleep, balanced meals, and moderate exercise as essential parts of overall wellness.
5. **Boundaries for Loved Ones:** Helping friends or family learn when to say "no," how to respond to manipulative statements, and when to seek their own counseling.

Building Healthier Coping Methods

For a person with narcissistic traits, acknowledging that they are not always right or invincible can be a big hurdle. Yet, learning healthier coping skills can ease their physical and emotional stress. Examples include:

- **Problem-Solving Skills:** Instead of reacting with anger, pause to identify the real issue, consider options, and choose a reasonable course of action.
- **Self-Reflection Journals:** Writing down daily challenges or conflicts, noting personal feelings, can reveal patterns they did not see before.

- **Goal-Setting for Health:** Creating goals that are not just about appearance—like wanting to move more for better heart health instead of only seeking admiration for muscles—can shift the focus from shallow reasons to real wellness.
- **Mindful Moments:** Taking a few minutes each day to be quiet, breathe slowly, and observe thoughts without acting on them can lower stress. This might feel strange at first for someone who constantly seeks action or attention, but it can become a calming habit.

Healing for Those Affected

Loved ones, colleagues, and friends who have been drained by a self-obsessed person's behavior might need their own path to healing. They could try:

- **Therapy or Support Groups:** Sharing experiences with others who understand can lift the sense of isolation.
- **Boundary-Setting Workshops:** Some counseling centers offer sessions on how to set and maintain personal limits.
- **Personal Stress-Relief Activities:** Regular walks, light workouts, art, reading, or other hobbies that help reduce tension.
- **Talking to Trusted Allies:** Having at least one friend or relative who knows the situation can help them feel less alone.

Recognizing Patterns Early

Catching the signs of narcissistic behavior and its stress-related fallout early can prevent larger health crises. If someone notices they are constantly tired, in conflict, or feeling that nothing is ever enough to satisfy them, they might benefit from talking with a mental health professional. Early intervention is often easier than waiting until severe emotional or physical harm sets in.

Breaking the Cycle

One core challenge is that the narcissistic individual might not see any reason to change. They could blame people around them, saying their stress is caused by incompetent coworkers, a rude partner, or a world that does not appreciate them. This mindset stops them from seeking help. In such cases, external events—a job loss, a breakup, or a major health scare—might serve as a wake-up call. That crisis might push them to admit their approach is causing real harm.

If they do reach that point, there is a chance to break the cycle. Recognizing the link between self-centered habits and harmful stress or health problems can open the door to genuine growth. By learning to manage stress, share praise, accept feedback, and empathize with others, they can reduce the emotional swings that damage both mind and body.

Hope for Improvement

While the physical and emotional consequences linked to narcissism can be serious, improvement is possible if a person is willing to look inward. Making these changes requires consistent effort over time. It may involve:

- Studying resources about healthy emotional regulation
- Facing the reality of mistakes and apologizing when needed
- Building a routine that includes rest and stress management
- Learning to take pleasure in small, meaningful successes rather than chasing grand displays

It is not an overnight shift. But with dedication, someone who has lived under the weight of self-obsession can discover a more balanced way of being. They may find that they feel better physically and emotionally, enjoy calmer relationships, and gain a steadier sense of self.

Conclusion

Narcissism does not only hurt relationships and social connections—it can also lead to a range of physical and emotional troubles for both the self-obsessed individual and those around them. Chronic stress, anger outbursts, and a lack of healthy self-care can result in headaches, digestive problems, fatigue, or more serious conditions over time. Loved ones can suffer from anxiety, "burnout by association," and the emotional rollercoaster that the narcissistic person creates.

Even so, there are paths to lessen these harms. By seeking professional support, learning better ways to handle stress, and respecting boundaries in relationships, it is possible to manage or reduce the damaging effects of a self-obsessed lifestyle. This shift can lead to improved health, stronger relationships, and a more stable sense of self-worth. In the next chapter, we will look at how to recognize harmful behavior more directly, pointing out clear warning signs and when it might be time to step away or seek outside help. Understanding these signals can help people protect themselves and respond in a thoughtful manner.

CHAPTER 16: RECOGNIZING HARMFUL BEHAVIOR

Throughout this book, we have explored the nature of narcissism—what it looks like, how it grows, and its effects on different parts of life. One crucial topic is how to spot harmful behavior in a self-obsessed individual. Not every instance of vanity or bragging points to a major problem. But when certain signs show up repeatedly, they can indicate that the person's behavior has reached a point where it is hurting others or even breaking rules. In this chapter, we will learn what these red flags are, how to tell if a line is being crossed, and what steps to consider if you find yourself in a situation with someone displaying these worrying traits.

Differentiating Annoying from Dangerous

Sometimes, we deal with narcissistic people who brag or demand attention but do not pose serious harm. They might be irritating, but they are not necessarily abusive. Other times, a self-focused person can cross into emotional or physical harm, leaving deep scars. Understanding the difference helps us respond in proportion to the situation.

- **Mild Annoyance:** The individual might be boastful at social events, hog discussions, or fish for praise often. They rarely show empathy, but they do not threaten or terrorize others.
- **Moderate Concern:** The person frequently lies, manipulates, or shows mood swings that create a stressful environment. They might shame or blame others a lot, creating emotional strain.
- **Severe Harm or Danger:** The person may isolate a partner from friends or family, use threats or violence, engage in financial abuse, or control every aspect of another's life. This can escalate to emotional or physical harm that puts a person's well-being at risk.

Each level calls for a different approach. Mild annoyances might be managed by setting boundaries or reducing contact. Severe harm requires stronger actions, such as seeking professional help, legal protection, or leaving the environment entirely.

Warning Signs of Emotional Abuse

Emotional abuse involves patterns that hurt a person's mental or emotional health. A self-obsessed individual can be emotionally abusive by:

1. **Gaslighting:** Denying facts, events, or the other person's perception, making them question their own reality.
2. **Constant Criticism:** Putting down someone's appearance, efforts, or intelligence to keep them feeling inferior.
3. **Excessive Control:** Deciding who the other person can see, where they can go, or how they spend money.
4. **Isolation:** Discouraging or blocking the other person from visiting friends or family.
5. **Threats of Abandonment or Harm:** Saying things like, "I'll leave you if you don't do this," or "You'll regret it if you go against me."

These methods keep the self-obsessed person in power while the other individual feels trapped or confused. If you observe these signals in a relationship—yours or someone else's—it could be a sign of serious abuse, not just selfishness.

Detecting Financial Exploitation

Financial abuse or exploitation can appear in various ways. A narcissistic individual might insist that their partner or family member give them money for expensive items or pay their bills. They could push the idea that they deserve certain luxuries and that others should provide them. Over time, they might drain bank accounts, take control of assets, or put the other person in debt.

In a workplace, a self-obsessed boss might order staff to run personal errands on company time or mislead clients for higher profits. These actions can point to unethical or illegal conduct. Recognizing the behavior early allows employees or partners to protect themselves or report the wrongdoing to the right authorities.

Physical or Sexual Intimidation

While not all narcissistic people resort to physical harm, those who do can become quite dangerous. Warning signs include:

- **Pushing, Shoving, or Threatening Touch:** Using physical force during arguments or as a way to show dominance.
- **Blocking Exits:** Standing in a doorway to prevent someone from leaving a room, especially during disagreements.
- **Forced Intimacy:** Pressuring or forcing sexual contact when the other person says "no."
- **Threatening Looks or Gestures:** Using a menacing stare, raised fist, or throwing objects near the other person.

Any form of physical intimidation is a severe red flag. It goes beyond normal conflict and can signal potential for real violence. Experts advise seeking help from friends, family, a hotline, or law enforcement if you suspect physical harm is possible.

The Role of Public Image vs. Private Behavior

One tricky aspect of self-obsessed individuals who cross the line into harm is that they might maintain a charming public image. They can appear polite, helpful, or even community-minded to neighbors or coworkers. Yet, behind closed doors, they might show a darker side—raging at partners, insulting family members, or controlling finances. This contrast can make it hard for outsiders to believe a victim's account if the narcissistic person appears so pleasant in public.

"Split" Personalities

This split can leave victims feeling isolated. They might try to tell friends or relatives about the abuser's behavior, only to be met with disbelief. The abuser may even claim the victim is the one with problems. Being aware that a person's public face might differ from their private one is important when evaluating accusations of harm.

Consistent Pattern Over Time

A key factor in recognizing harmful narcissistic behavior is whether there is a consistent pattern. A single angry outburst, though still concerning, might not define a person as abusive. However, repeated acts of control, belittling, or aggression show a pattern. If you see the same behaviors happening week after week or month after month, that is a sign the individual has a deeper problem rather than just a bad day.

Apologies That Do Not Bring Change

Some self-obsessed people might apologize after an outburst or harmful act, promising to do better. But if they continue to repeat the same actions, the apologies might serve only to calm things momentarily. Over time, this cycle can become so familiar that the victim begins to doubt whether change is really possible. Observing the follow-through—or lack of it—after an apology can indicate whether someone is actually trying to be better.

Signs You Are in a Harmful Dynamic

It can be tough to see clearly if you are the one in a relationship with a harmful, self-obsessed person. Some signs include:

1. **Feeling Constantly on Edge:** You tiptoe around certain topics, fears, or opinions to avoid conflict.
2. **Loss of Personal Identity:** You might notice you no longer pursue hobbies or friendships you once loved because they upset or anger the narcissistic individual.
3. **Walking in Fear of Emotional Reactions:** You may keep secrets or lie to avoid the other person's extreme anger or scorn.
4. **Thinking You Are at Fault for Everything:** The self-obsessed partner might twist events so you feel guilty all the time.
5. **Frequent Emotional Highs and Lows:** Brief moments of approval or kindness keep you attached, but the rest of the time you feel confused, hurt, or worried.

If these feelings dominate your daily life, it might signal that the other person has crossed a serious boundary, and you might need outside help to regain control of your situation.

Steps to Take If You Suspect Harm

1. **Document Incidents:** Keep a simple log of dates, times, and what happened—especially in cases of threats, physical aggression, or major manipulation. This record can be valuable for your own clarity or if you decide to seek legal action.
2. **Reach Out for Support:** Speak to a trusted friend, family member, or counselor. Describe what is happening. If you feel unsafe, consider contacting a helpline or local community resource.
3. **Protect Personal Information:** If finances are in question, secure your bank accounts, change passwords, and consider storing sensitive documents in a safe place.
4. **Plan for Safety:** In cases of possible physical danger, having a plan to leave quickly can be lifesaving. This might include arranging a safe place to stay or having a friend "on call."
5. **Seek Professional Advice:** Lawyers, support groups, or therapists can give tips specific to your location and situation. They can advise on restraining orders, child custody issues, or ways to cope with emotional trauma.

When Children Are Involved

The situation becomes more complex if children are part of a household with a harmful narcissistic adult. Children rely on parents or guardians for protection, so they are especially vulnerable if one parent is abusive. The other parent or a concerned relative might need to take action, which can include:

- **Contacting Child Protective Services:** If a child is being harmed or witnessing severe abuse, authorities might step in to ensure their safety.
- **Seeking Therapy for the Child:** A counselor can help children process what they have seen or experienced.
- **Documenting Incidents Affecting Children:** Keep notes on any events where the child is threatened, yelled at, or used as a way to hurt the other parent.
- **Custody and Visitation Decisions:** Courts may limit contact or require supervised visits if the abusive behavior is putting the child at risk.

It can be a tough path, but protecting a child's well-being must come first.

Spotting Harm at Work

A self-obsessed boss or coworker can create a hostile environment that goes beyond just being unpleasant. Signs of crossing a harmful boundary at work include:

- **Bullying:** Repeated insults, sabotage, or humiliation in front of others.
- **Discrimination:** Targeting certain employees unfairly due to race, gender, disability, or other factors.
- **Unfair Workload:** Piling tasks on someone as punishment or to watch them fail.
- **Threats About Job Security:** Using the risk of firing or demotion as a tool to keep employees silent or obedient.

If such behaviors occur, one can speak with Human Resources (if available), keep written records of incidents, and possibly consult an employment lawyer if the company fails to address the issues. It is important not to ignore severe harassment in a job setting, as it can harm both mental and physical health.

Cyber Harassment and Online Threats

Technology has opened new avenues for narcissistic individuals to hurt others. They might:

- **Flood Someone with Aggressive Messages:** Bombarding texts or social media accounts with insults or threats.
- **Spread Private Information or Photos:** Posting embarrassing personal details to shame or control the other person.
- **Fake Accounts and Stalking:** Using multiple profiles to follow or harass someone online.
- **Cut Off Digital Access:** If they share an account or control the home internet, they might restrict the other person's usage to isolate them.

These actions can be serious and might break cyberbullying or harassment laws in many regions. Victims should keep screenshots or logs of incidents and consider reporting them to the platform, service provider, or law enforcement, depending on severity.

Knowing Your Rights and Options

If you realize the other person's behavior is more than just unpleasant—that it is abusive or illegal—you have rights. Depending on the location, laws may allow you to file for restraining orders, press charges, or seek compensation for harm done. You might speak with a legal service or an advocacy group to find out what steps are allowed in your area. This process can feel intimidating, especially if the narcissistic individual is forceful or well-connected, but no one should be trapped in a harmful situation because they think they have no legal options.

Emotional Challenges in Leaving or Confronting

Confronting or leaving a harmful, self-focused person is not simple. There can be emotional attachments, financial dependencies, or fear of retaliation. Sometimes, the narcissistic individual may show brief kindness just when their partner or victim considers leaving, pulling them back in. This is sometimes referred to as a "honeymoon phase," which confuses the victim into thinking change is real.

Guilt and Hope

Victims can feel guilty, as though they are abandoning someone who "needs" them. They might also still hope the abusive person will turn into the ideal partner or friend they saw glimpses of early on. But repeated patterns of harm often do not vanish without major intervention. Therapy for the abuser might help if they commit fully, but that is not guaranteed. Facing the reality of the situation can be emotionally difficult, yet it is an essential step toward safety.

Seeking Professional Help

If you or someone close to you notices these harmful patterns, it is wise to contact a professional. This could be a counselor, a doctor, or an organization specializing in domestic violence or workplace harassment. Professionals are trained to spot signs of abuse and guide people through the steps they can take. They can also offer emotional support, which is key during such a stressful time.

Even if the narcissistic person refuses help, you can seek it for yourself. Learning coping methods, building self-confidence, and planning for your safety are all within your control. A trained therapist can also help you process any guilt, fear, or anger you feel, making it easier to move forward and rebuild a healthier life.

Educating Yourself and Others

Knowledge is power. Understanding the signs of dangerous narcissistic behavior can protect you from falling into harmful relationships. It can also help you spot trouble in a friend's life before it becomes too severe. Sharing what you know with others in a careful way—while respecting privacy and boundaries—can create a supportive network that stands against abuse.

In addition, schools and community groups can hold talks on healthy relationships, teaching people to recognize harmful behavior early. The more people know, the harder it becomes for a self-centered abuser to operate in secret. If communities come together to speak openly about emotional control, bullying, or violence, they can create an environment less tolerant of these acts.

Boundaries, Exit Plans, and New Beginnings

If you decide a relationship or situation is harmful, setting boundaries is a first step. This might involve refusing to engage in certain topics, limiting contact, or seeking an outside mediator. In more extreme cases, leaving might be the only path. That could mean moving out, filing legal papers, or changing jobs. These moves can be scary, especially if the narcissistic individual tries to retaliate. But staying in a harmful environment often leads to more damage, emotionally and physically.

After exiting a harmful relationship or workplace, people often find they need time to heal. They might feel relief mixed with sadness or guilt. They may worry about the future, especially if the narcissistic individual tries to make contact again. Support from friends, family, or counselors is vital during this phase. Over time, many people discover that being free from constant fear or manipulation allows them to regain confidence, explore personal interests, and form healthier connections.

Conclusion

Recognizing harmful narcissistic behavior is critical for anyone who might find themselves in its path. Red flags such as emotional abuse, physical intimidation, financial exploitation, and isolation can appear gradually or suddenly. By knowing what to watch for—repeated patterns of control, gaslighting, blame shifting, or threats—you can better protect yourself and those you care about.

No one should have to live in fear or surrender their well-being to a self-obsessed abuser. Whether the situation involves a personal relationship, a workplace, or an online platform, there are steps to take to reduce the harm. Documenting incidents, seeking professional support, and building a strong circle of allies can make a big difference. It may not be an easy road, but leaving behind or setting firm limits with a dangerous narcissistic individual can open the door to a safer, healthier life.

In the upcoming chapters, we will explore ways to address the problem of self-obsession, including strategies for change and how to handle a narcissistic person in day-to-day life. Understanding how to react wisely and protect ourselves, as well as encouraging healthier behavior when possible, is key to reducing the negative impact of narcissism in our personal circles and beyond.

CHAPTER 17: APPROACHES TO ADDRESS THE PROBLEM

By this point, we have seen how self-obsessed behavior can cause conflict in relationships, families, workplaces, and personal well-being. Knowing the harm is one thing; figuring out how to address it is another. In this chapter, we will look at concrete methods people can use to deal with narcissistic traits—both in themselves and in those around them. We will explore a range of options, from therapy and counseling to self-guided steps. Our goal is to show that while self-centered habits can be tough to break, change is possible when approached with clarity, patience, and the right tools.

Understanding the Scope of Change

Before diving into specific methods, it is important to note that not everyone who displays narcissistic behavior is willing or able to change. Some might not see a problem at all. Others might feel a deep sense of shame hidden under their pride, making them defensive or fearful of self-reflection. As a result, the person's openness to facing their behavior plays a huge role in how successful any approach can be.

At the same time, people dealing with narcissism from the outside—like friends or family—often wonder if there is a path to improvement. They may try many tactics, from gentle persuasion to tough ultimatums. Each method has its place, and different approaches might work better for different individuals. In some cases, leaving or limiting contact could be the only safe and healthy option. In others, empathy and clear boundaries might encourage slow but genuine growth.

Therapy and Professional Support

One of the most direct ways to tackle narcissism is through therapy or counseling. A trained therapist can help a person see the roots of their self-focused behavior. They might explore childhood memories, pinpoint insecurities, or figure out why they feel the need to impress others. Over time, therapy can guide the individual to replace destructive thought patterns with healthier ones. Below are some common types of professional support:

1. **Individual Therapy:** In a private setting, the therapist and client can discuss feelings, relationships, and potential triggers. The therapist might use techniques from cognitive-behavioral therapy (CBT) to challenge unhelpful beliefs like "I must always be the best" or "No one else's opinion matters."
2. **Group Therapy or Support Groups:** Sometimes, hearing peers talk about similar struggles can help break the illusion of being alone or misunderstood. In group settings, each member can practice listening, empathy, and sharing the spotlight. However, a person with strong narcissistic traits might initially feel uncomfortable or see it as competition.
3. **Family Therapy:** If narcissistic behavior affects the entire household, family therapy can help everyone understand communication pitfalls and set new rules. It can be a space where each member states their needs, and the self-obsessed person sees the real impact of their actions.
4. **Couples Counseling:** In romantic relationships, a professional can guide discussions so the couple deals with recurring arguments or power imbalances. It can also help the partner of a narcissistic individual figure out clear boundaries and ensure their own voice is heard.

The Challenge of Acceptance

A key challenge is getting a narcissistic person to agree to therapy. Many fear judgment and do not want to admit faults. Some might attend only if threatened with divorce, job loss, or serious conflict. Even then, they could drop out when sessions dig too deep. Because of this, therapists sometimes emphasize small, specific goals—like learning to pause before blaming someone else or practicing empathy in structured exercises.

Setting Boundaries

For those who deal with a narcissistic individual—a partner, parent, sibling, coworker, or friend—one of the most powerful steps is setting firm boundaries.

When boundaries are clear and consistently followed, the self-focused person has less room to manipulate or dominate situations. Here are tips for creating effective boundaries:

1. **Be Direct and Specific:** Vague statements like "Stop being so selfish" rarely help. Instead, say, "I will end the conversation if you insult me," or "I will not lend you money anymore."
2. **Stay Calm and Consistent:** A narcissistic individual might test limits or react with anger to see if you give in. If you stay firm over time, they learn you mean what you say.
3. **Use "I" Statements:** Instead of launching accusations, focus on your own needs: "I need some quiet time right now," or "I need you to speak respectfully if we are to continue talking."
4. **Follow Through:** Boundaries without action mean little. If you say you will leave the room when they start yelling but then stay, the person might not respect your words next time.

Boundaries are not about punishing the other person. They are about protecting your own mental and emotional space. They let you interact without constantly being on guard. Over time, boundaries can sometimes teach the self-obsessed person that certain behaviors have consequences—something they might not have experienced if others always gave in.

Building Empathy

For those seeking to address their own narcissistic traits, learning empathy can be a crucial step. Empathy involves recognizing that others have feelings and needs that are just as valid as your own. While this may sound simple, someone used to focusing on themselves might find it difficult. They may have never practiced tuning in to the emotional states of others. Here are some approaches to build empathy:

- **Active Listening Exercises:** Practice listening to someone's story or complaint without interrupting, offering advice, or changing the topic. After they finish, repeat back what you heard to ensure you understand.

- **Perspective-Shifting:** Try imagining how someone else sees a situation. Ask, "If I were in their shoes, what would I feel?" This skill can be learned through role-play in therapy or by consciously pausing in everyday life.
- **Service or Volunteering:** Activities that help others in need—like working at a food bank or cleaning a community park—can offer a tangible sense of contributing beyond oneself. Over time, this may spark a more genuine respect for the struggles and achievements of others.

Practical Self-Reflection Tools

People with self-obsessed tendencies often avoid looking inward because they fear discovering flaws. In addressing narcissism, however, self-reflection is vital. Some methods to foster healthy self-awareness include:

1. **Journaling:** Write down conflicts or intense emotions. Note how you felt, what you said, and how the other person reacted. Reviewing these entries later can reveal patterns of blame, anger, or dismissive behavior that might otherwise go unnoticed.
2. **Mindfulness or Relaxation Techniques:** Simple breathing exercises or quiet reflection time can help break the cycle of constant self-assertion. Slowing down can open mental space for new insights.
3. **Personal Milestones:** Set goals that focus on improvement rather than external praise—like calmly discussing a disagreement without raising your voice, or giving someone else credit in a team project. Recognize (avoid "celebrate") each success as a step toward a healthier way of relating.
4. **Asking for Feedback:** Though it can feel uncomfortable, asking trusted friends or loved ones for honest input can shine a light on blind spots. This requires a willingness to hear criticism without immediate defensiveness.

Changing Communication Styles

Addressing narcissism often involves shifting how people talk to each other. Communication skills can transform conflicts into chances for growth:

- **Calm, Clear Language:** Avoid name-calling, sarcasm, or shouting. These provoke defensiveness. Instead, speak directly about what is bothering you or what needs to change.
- **Focused Conversations:** A self-obsessed individual might derail talks by wandering into bragging or shifting blame. Gently steer the discussion back to the main issue. If needed, restate the problem: "Right now, we are talking about how you yelled at me in front of our coworkers."
- **Small Agreements:** Instead of trying to solve massive issues all at once, aim for smaller points of agreement. This can build momentum. For instance, "We both agree we want a respectful environment. So can we agree that name-calling is off-limits?"
- **Scheduled Talks:** Emotions can run high if serious discussions happen randomly. Scheduling a talk—such as deciding to sit down calmly after work—gives both sides time to prepare. This can prevent snap arguments fueled by stress.

Involving Neutral Mediators

When direct conversations fail, involving a neutral third party can help. This might be a professional mediator, a respected family friend, or a community leader. Their role is not to blame one side or the other but to make sure each person's viewpoint is heard. Mediators can help:

- **Define Problems Clearly:** They encourage both parties to name specific issues and events, rather than making broad accusations.
- **Keep Emotions in Check:** If tempers rise, the mediator can pause the discussion, reminding everyone of the goal—finding workable solutions.
- **Suggest Fair Compromises:** A skilled mediator might see win-win paths neither side considered.
- **Hold Each Side Accountable:** Mediators can remind the self-obsessed person when they are dominating the dialogue, or prompt the other person to speak up if they typically stay silent.

Not every narcissistic individual will agree to mediation, but if they are willing, it can create a more balanced environment than conversations that happen unmonitored.

Digital and Social Media Boundaries

In our online-driven world, narcissistic behavior can appear on social platforms as constant posting, picking fights, or seeking endless likes. Addressing these habits means setting limits online as well:

- **Time Limits for Social Apps:** Reducing the hours spent comparing likes or crafting the perfect post can lower the push for external approval.
- **Content Choices:** Encouraging a shift away from purely self-focused material. For example, posting a short reflection on something learned or highlighting someone else's achievement.
- **Mindful Interaction:** Instead of instantly replying to critics or engaging in arguments, learn to step back. Ask, "Am I truly listening or just defending myself?"
- **Privacy Adjustments:** Tightening who can view posts or comment might reduce the temptation to flaunt personal accomplishments or get into spats with strangers.

Educating Children and Teens

If narcissistic behavior is caught early, there is a better chance of guiding children or teens onto a healthier path. Parents, teachers, and mentors can:

- **Model Balanced Praise:** Highlight genuine effort and improvement rather than calling the child the "best" at everything.
- **Encourage Empathy:** Ask how they think their actions affect others. Invite them to help siblings or classmates.
- **Teach Conflict Skills:** Show them how to handle disagreements without name-calling or shutting others down.
- **Reward Teamwork:** Give attention to sharing, helping, and group problem-solving, so they see that mutual success can be just as rewarding as being solo in the spotlight.

Children who learn these lessons may be less likely to develop hardened self-centered habits later. Early intervention can be a game-changer.

Workplace Strategies

In a job setting, addressing narcissism can be complex due to power structures. Still, certain strategies can help:

1. **Clear Guidelines and Job Descriptions:** When roles and tasks are spelled out, it is harder for a self-focused coworker to claim credit for someone else's work.
2. **Feedback Loops:** Regular performance reviews that include peer feedback can highlight cooperation and respectful communication as key metrics.
3. **Team-Based Recognition:** Praising or rewarding entire groups for successes can lessen the appeal of one person hogging the spotlight.
4. **HR Intervention:** If a narcissistic employee crosses the line into bullying or abuse, formal procedures may be needed. Documentation of incidents is essential here.

A supportive workplace culture that values fairness, shared goals, and respect can limit the negative impact of self-obsession. Leaders who embody humility and inclusion set a strong example for all employees.

Handling Setbacks and Relapses

Change is rarely smooth. A self-obsessed person might make progress—listening more, blaming less—then revert during stressful times. Loved ones or coworkers can feel discouraged if these relapses happen frequently. However, setbacks can be part of the growth process. Some tips include:

- **Acknowledge Small Wins:** If the person handled a conflict calmly, note it, even if other issues remain. Positive reinforcement can encourage them to keep trying.
- **Stay Firm on Boundaries:** Do not relax essential limits just because they improved for a while. Consistency remains key.
- **Offer Constructive Reminders:** Gently say, "It seems you're reverting to old habits. Remember how well it went when we tried to solve problems together?"
- **Avoid Shaming:** Extreme criticism might push them into defense mode. Aim for balanced input, pointing out what changed for the better and what still needs work.

When to Step Away

In some cases, despite all efforts, the narcissistic individual refuses change or becomes more harmful over time. Loved ones or colleagues might need to protect themselves by stepping away. This can be emotionally painful, especially in close relationships, but staying in a toxic situation can damage mental and physical health. Knowing when to leave a job or end a personal connection is a tough call, but might be necessary if:

- **Abuse Escalates:** Verbal attacks become physical threats or severe control tactics.
- **No Accountability:** The person never admits wrongdoing, or any apologies are followed by the same behavior.
- **Endless Conflict:** The stress overshadows any benefit of the relationship, and outside help is consistently refused.
- **Personal Well-Being Declines:** You find yourself anxious or depressed most days, even away from the person.

Though stepping away may not fix the narcissistic behavior, it can allow you to heal and avoid further harm.

Hope and Realistic Expectations

While dramatic transformations can happen, they are not guaranteed. Addressing narcissism is often a slow journey that requires:

- **Honest Self-Examination:** The individual needs to accept they have areas to improve.
- **Steady Effort Over Time:** Quick fixes tend to fail. It takes months or years of practice to replace ingrained attitudes.
- **A Support System:** Family, friends, or counselors who offer both encouragement and truth.
- **Personal Motivation:** The desire to change must come from within. It might be sparked by a major life event or ongoing dissatisfaction with how relationships are going.

Some do manage to dial back their self-centered focus, learning to share credit, listen openly, and own their mistakes. Their relationships can grow closer. They might become more grounded and discover new interests beyond seeking praise. Others may only change in small ways or not at all. Recognizing that outcome is not entirely in your hands can bring a sense of acceptance.

Conclusion

Dealing with narcissism—whether it is your own or someone else's—can be deeply challenging. Yet, there are concrete approaches to address the problem:

- **Professional Support:** Therapy, counseling, or mediation can shine light on hidden insecurities and teach new behaviors.
- **Boundaries and Communication:** Clear rules, patient dialogue, and consistent follow-through can limit harm and encourage respect.
- **Self-Reflection and Empathy-Building:** Tools like journaling, mindfulness, and volunteering help replace vanity with a more open outlook.
- **Workplace and Family Strategies:** Structures that reward teamwork and fairness can prevent a self-obsessed person from dominating or harming others.
- **Realistic Goals and Persistence:** Change is slow. Setbacks happen. But small improvements can add up over time if the individual is willing to keep trying.

If all else fails, or if the relationship becomes abusive, stepping away might be the healthiest option. No one can fully control another person's choices, but we can control our responses and protect our well-being. This balanced understanding gives us a way forward, whether we attempt to foster growth in a narcissistic individual or decide to move on. In the next chapter, we will focus on day-to-day methods for handling a narcissist, from practical coping tactics to emotional self-care for those who share space or responsibilities with a self-obsessed person.

CHAPTER 18: HANDLING A NARCISSIST

Even if you understand the nature of narcissism and are aware of strategies for addressing the problem, it can still be difficult to interact with a self-obsessed person daily. Whether it is a boss, a partner, a friend, or a relative, their demands or behaviors might test your patience and well-being. This chapter focuses on specific ways to manage daily life around someone with narcissistic traits. We will cover communication tips, emotional survival tactics, and pointers for keeping your sense of self intact, no matter how challenging the situation.

Recognizing Your Role and Limits

Before going into specific techniques, it is essential to know that you cannot singlehandedly "fix" a narcissistic individual. They must decide to make changes themselves. Your role is to protect your own well-being, communicate effectively, and refuse to be pulled into harmful patterns. Accepting that your power has limits can actually bring a sense of relief. It helps you release the burden of trying to force someone to become different.

Communication Tactics

1. **Stay Grounded and Polite:** When talking with a self-focused person, keep your voice calm. If they raise theirs, do not match their volume. Show you are in control of your emotions. This can sometimes reduce tension.
2. **Use Clear Statements:** Make requests or set boundaries in short, simple sentences. Long explanations might give them room to interrupt or twist your words. For example, "I need to leave now. I'll talk to you tomorrow," is direct and leaves little room for argument.
3. **Avoid Trigger Words:** Labeling someone as "narcissistic" during an argument can cause immediate defensiveness. Instead, stick to describing behavior: "When you keep interrupting me, I feel unheard."
4. **Focus on Issues, Not Character Attacks:** If you must address a problem, highlight the event or action rather than calling them lazy or selfish. "When you missed the meeting, the rest of us had to cover your tasks," is better than, "You're too self-absorbed to show up."

5. **Do Not Argue Over Facts You Can Prove Elsewhere:** If they deny something that happened, consider calmly pointing them to written records, emails, or neutral witnesses. Avoid lengthy back-and-forth. Show the evidence and move on.

Emotional Boundaries and Self-Care

Being around a narcissistic person can be draining. Setting emotional boundaries means deciding what you will and will not absorb. Consider these steps:

1. **Give Yourself Time to Decompress:** After a tense interaction, take a short walk or do a quick activity you find calming. This helps prevent carrying stress into the rest of your day.
2. **Limit Personal Sharing:** A self-obsessed individual might use your personal stories as ammo in arguments or gossip. Be selective about what you reveal.
3. **Lean on a Support Network:** Regularly talk with friends or family who validate your feelings. Knowing others see what you are dealing with can keep you from doubting yourself.
4. **Practice Positive Self-Talk:** Remind yourself that their behavior is about them, not you. If they try to belittle you, recall your own accomplishments, values, and healthy relationships.
5. **Plan "Safe Exits":** If you feel an interaction is spiraling into conflict, politely excuse yourself: "I need to handle something now. Let's revisit this later." This can prevent you from being cornered.

Redirecting Conversations

Narcissistic people often steer discussions back to themselves. This can be exhausting if you need to talk about shared tasks or decisions. Try these methods:

- **Use Their Name or Title:** Start with, "Chris, I understand you have ideas. Let's take a moment to review the plan we agreed on." This personal address might grab their attention.

- **Offer a Limited Praise, Then Shift Topic:** For instance, "Yes, your approach to last week's project was creative. Now, we need to decide who will handle the budget next quarter." This acknowledges them before returning to the main subject.
- **Set a Conversation Agenda:** If possible, have a written list of points to cover. If they wander off-track, gently bring them back: "That's interesting, but we're here to finalize the shipping schedule."
- **Ask Direct Questions:** Sometimes, guiding them with targeted queries can keep them from rambling. Example: "How many units do you propose we send first?" or "What date works best for you?"

Handling Criticism and Blame

Narcissistic individuals often avoid blame, pinning problems on others. If you find yourself accused unfairly:

1. **Stay Calm in the Moment:** Arguing immediately might escalate things. Instead, respond with something like, "I'd like to talk about that calmly. Let's figure out the facts."
2. **Collect Evidence:** If it is a work issue, keep emails or chat records. If it is a household matter, note dates and times of events. Clear evidence can show the truth if needed later.
3. **Avoid Counter-Attacks:** If you respond by insulting them, the discussion can blow up. Stay on topic: "Let's check the project log. It shows who submitted what and when."
4. **Propose a Solution:** If they claim you messed up, and you do see some fault on your side, own it but invite collaboration: "I'll correct my part. Can you also handle the pieces you were assigned?"

Deflecting Manipulation

A self-obsessed person might try to manipulate you with guilt, flattery, or veiled threats. Being prepared can lessen the impact:

- **Recognize the Pattern:** If they only flatter you when they want a favor, see it for what it is—transactional praise.

- **Delay Big Decisions:** If they push you to agree immediately, say, "I need to think this over. Let's talk tomorrow." This gives you time to consult others or clear your head.
- **Stay Neutral in Tone:** If they sense you are upset, they might intensify their tactics. Keep a calm voice, showing their attempts are not rattling you.
- **Repeat Your Boundary or Statement:** They may try to make you forget your stance. Return to the core point: "I understand you want that, but I can't give it. My decision is final."

When You Must Collaborate

Working with a narcissistic teammate or living with a self-focused family member might mean you cannot simply walk away. Here are tips to survive and function:

1. **Divide Tasks Clearly:** Assign each person's responsibilities in writing so there is less room for blame-shifting.
2. **Hold Short, Structured Meetings:** Keep agendas tight. Ask for input in a clear order. Summarize decisions at the end to avoid future confusion.
3. **Document Agreements:** After any big discussion, send an email confirming the points settled: "Just to confirm, you will handle X, and I will handle Y."
4. **Use "We" Language if Possible:** Emphasize how each step supports the team or family: "We need to do this to meet the deadline," rather than, "You must do this because I said so."
5. **Small Wins as a Group:** If something goes well, give credit to everyone involved. This can reduce their urge to claim full credit.

Dealing with Public Scenes

Some narcissistic people like making a spectacle, turning any disagreement into a big show if others are watching. To handle this:

- **Stay Calm and Low-Key:** Respond softly rather than raising your voice. This contrast can make the scene less dramatic.
- **Suggest a Private Discussion:** "Let's step aside and talk privately so we don't disturb everyone." This removes their public audience.
- **End it if Needed:** If they refuse to calm down, you can quietly leave. Staying put could fuel them further. Let them know you are happy to talk later when it is calmer.

Handling Emotional Manipulation in Personal Relationships

In close relationships, a self-obsessed partner might use emotional tactics like the silent treatment, extreme jealousy, or guilt-tripping. To cope:

1. **Name the Behavior Quietly:** If they shut down and ignore you, calmly say, "I notice you are not speaking. Is there a reason?" This shows you recognize what they are doing.
2. **Refuse to Play the Game:** If they demand you chase after them or beg for forgiveness, avoid that pattern. Invite open communication but do not reward silent treatment with extra attention.
3. **Stand Up for Your Own Time:** If they insist you stay home rather than see friends, politely but firmly keep your social plans. "I understand you don't want me to go, but I'll be back at 9 p.m."
4. **Use "Bridging" Phrases:** Sometimes, acknowledging a small part of their point can cool things down. "I see you're upset that I was late. I'm sorry for the delay, but I still want to understand why you're so angry."

Protecting Your Self-Worth

Long-term exposure to narcissistic behavior can chip away at your self-esteem. Combat this effect by:

- **Creating Personal Goals:** Spend time each day on interests or skills that build your confidence, like writing, painting, playing a sport, or learning a new hobby.

- **Keeping a Log of Kind Moments:** Note down the times you helped others or achieved something. Reflecting on these entries can counter any negative messages from the self-focused person.
- **Seeking Encouragement Elsewhere:** Stay connected with friends or groups that value mutual respect. Join clubs, volunteer, or talk online with supportive communities.
- **Refusing to Compare Yourself:** A narcissistic person might boast of their possessions, achievements, or popularity. Remind yourself that their self-worth measurements do not have to be yours.

Collaborating on Possible Change

If the narcissistic individual shows some willingness to grow, you can attempt small joint exercises:

- **Reflective Listening Sessions:** Agree that each person gets five minutes to speak without interruption, then the other repeats back what was said to ensure understanding.
- **Shared Goal-Setting:** Plan a small improvement project together, such as organizing a family event. Each of you outlines tasks, deadlines, and mutual support methods.
- **Reward Empathy Efforts:** If you notice them genuinely asking about your day or giving credit where due, mention how you appreciate that consideration. Positive feedback can reinforce better habits.

However, do not rely solely on these efforts. Professional guidance—like couple's counseling or family therapy—often goes further in reshaping deep-set patterns.

Knowing When You Need Distance

Sometimes, no strategy can fix the day-to-day strain of living or working with a deeply narcissistic individual. You might decide to limit or end contact if:

- **Your Well-Being Erodes:** You feel constantly anxious, depressed, or drained.

- **Boundaries Are Ignored:** Despite repeated attempts, they do not respect your needs or safety.
- **Abuse or Threats Escalate:** Verbal or physical aggression puts you at risk.
- **They Show No Desire to Improve:** All efforts fall flat, and continuing is too destructive.

Taking distance can be partial—limiting visits or phone calls—or complete if the situation is severe. This choice can bring guilt or sadness, but sometimes it is necessary to protect yourself.

Building a Supportive Environment

Whether you choose to stay in contact with the narcissistic person or step away, a strong support system can keep you grounded:

- **Friends and Family Who Understand:** Share what you are going through so they can offer encouragement and a listening ear.
- **Counseling or Support Groups:** Hearing from others who have managed similar situations can give new perspectives and coping tips.
- **Educational Resources:** Books, articles, and reputable online forums can help you stay informed and avoid blaming yourself.
- **Healthy Outlets:** Physical exercise, creative hobbies, or spiritual practices (if that fits your beliefs) can relieve stress built up from tense encounters.

Over time, building a life outside the narcissistic dynamic helps you see that their view of you is not the only one. You have worth and a future that goes beyond this one challenging relationship.

Accepting Realistic Outcomes

You might do everything "right" when handling a narcissist—using calm communication, setting boundaries, offering empathy. Yet, they still might resist or only change slightly. It is essential to accept that you have limited control. Your well-being does not hinge on fixing them. It hinges on managing your own responses and choices. Sometimes that means enduring small daily interactions while protecting your peace. Other times, it means moving on altogether.

Remember that growth is still possible. Some narcissistic individuals do improve their behavior if they face enough consequences or develop enough insight. Even moderate shifts—like apologizing occasionally or letting others speak more—can relieve tension. But any real change takes consistent effort from them. You can encourage it, but you cannot force it.

Conclusion

Handling a narcissist in daily life can feel like walking a tightrope. On one side, you want to maintain your own sense of respect and sanity. On the other, you need workable ways to communicate and collaborate. The tactics outlined here—calm communication, firm boundaries, selective sharing, evidence-based discussions, and self-care—can lessen the strain. They help you avoid being pulled into endless arguments or self-doubt.

Still, there are moments when leaving a job, limiting contact, or ending a relationship is the safest route. Each person's decision depends on the severity of the narcissist's behavior, the impact on everyday life, and the resources available for support. Whether you aim to keep working alongside them, preserve a family tie, or step away completely, the central theme is to protect your well-being. That means recognizing you cannot change another person's core outlook by sheer force of will. But you can shape the environment and interactions in ways that guard your peace of mind.

In our next chapters, we will look ahead at potential future impacts of narcissism on society as a whole and ways we might prepare for or limit its spread. We will also turn our attention to a final reflection on self-obsessed behavior, reminding ourselves why understanding and addressing it matters not just for personal relationships, but for the broader community we all share.

CHAPTER 19: POTENTIAL FUTURE IMPACTS OF NARCISSISM

Narcissism is not just an isolated trait that affects only individuals and their immediate circles. The spread of self-obsessed behavior can also impact society on a larger scale. This chapter explores how rising levels of narcissism might shape our communities, workplaces, schools, and cultural trends in the years ahead. We will discuss the potential costs—both emotional and practical—if self-centered outlooks become more common. At the same time, we will consider possible responses and ways to encourage healthier social norms that help balance personal ambition with empathy.

Shifting Social Norms

Modern life, with its emphasis on personal branding and online presence, sometimes rewards people who stand out, speak loudly, and draw attention to themselves. In a world where clicks and views can translate into influence or income, self-promotion may appear beneficial. Over time, this can shift social norms toward praising self-centered traits. For instance, young people might see that being loud or boastful online wins more followers and start to see such behavior as normal.

If this pattern continues, we may notice:

1. **Increased Competition Over Cooperation:** Groups or communities could shift toward a "me first" mentality, with less emphasis on collaboration. Instead of team achievements, people might focus on personal success and status, weakening mutual trust.
2. **Disregard for Shared Responsibilities:** When self-image dominates one's mind, tasks that benefit the group—like following community rules or volunteering for group projects—may lose priority. This could undermine collective goals.
3. **More Celebrity-Centric Culture:** With people looking to influencers or big personalities for role models, substance might take a back seat. A polished image might matter more than actual knowledge, experience, or integrity.

4. **Widening Gap in Relationships:** As bragging or vanity become widespread, genuine connections may become rarer. People who desire authentic friendships or partnerships might feel left out of a scene that rewards surface-level charm or shallow updates.

These changes do not imply that all hope is lost. Many individuals still appreciate kindness, humility, and the ability to see beyond oneself. However, if narcissistic behavior gains more acceptance, it can tilt the balance in everyday interactions, creating a world where self-glorification overshadows empathy.

Workplace Challenges and Economic Effects

Narcissism can also reshape the workplace. In competitive industries—like finance, technology, or entertainment—self-promoters might rise quickly, showcasing confidence and bold ideas. However, such environments risk promoting a culture where the loudest or flashiest voices take precedence over genuine teamwork or long-term planning. Possible outcomes include:

1. **High Employee Turnover:** If more leaders display self-centered traits, everyday staff might feel unvalued. They could leave, seeking workplaces with healthier cultures. The cost of replacing staff strains organizations, reducing overall productivity.
2. **Shallow Innovation:** Grand claims might overshadow careful research. A self-obsessed manager could rush projects to gain credit, ignoring steps that ensure quality. Over time, half-baked ideas might flood the market, wasting resources.
3. **Strained Leadership Pipelines:** If narcissistic styles become the norm among higher-ups, others who prefer collaboration may feel blocked from promotions. This can stifle diversity of thought and limit the range of skills in leadership roles.
4. **Risk of Scandals:** Self-focused executives might ignore ethical guidelines or manipulate finances to appear successful. Such behavior can bring legal trouble, damaging the company's reputation and finances.

On a broader economic level, an excess of short-term, showy decisions can undermine stability. Companies might chase quick wins rather than sustained growth. If entire industries adopt these habits, there could be cycles of booms and busts fueled by image-driven hype rather than solid performance.

Influence on Education and Youth Development

Classrooms and educational programs lay the foundation for future generations. If narcissistic attitudes become more widespread, schools might face new challenges. Some possible effects include:

1. **Focus on Performance Over Learning:** Teachers may notice students competing for the spotlight rather than developing deeper understanding. If children see that bragging about small achievements brings praise, they might put more effort into self-promotion than genuine study.
2. **Imbalanced Peer Relationships:** Children or teens with strong self-focused traits could dominate group projects or belittle peers. This environment can foster anxiety or resentment among classmates, breaking down unity in the classroom.
3. **Decreased Empathy Development:** School is a key place for children to practice social skills like sharing, listening, and showing kindness. If self-obsession is normalized, empathy lessons could fall behind, leaving some students poorly prepared for cooperative adult life.
4. **Parent-Teacher Conflicts:** Narcissistic parents might demand special treatment or blame teachers for any failure of their child. This can strain teacher-parent relationships and distract from the child's true needs.

Over time, youth raised in such conditions could emerge into adulthood lacking strong collaborative habits or conflict-resolution skills. This might translate into workplaces and communities where people clash often, find it hard to cooperate, and struggle to show understanding.

Technology Amplification

As technology advances, its effects on narcissistic tendencies may deepen. Social media and entertainment platforms already offer ways for individuals to chase likes, comments, and subscribers. In the future, new tech developments might add to this:

- **Virtual Reality Spaces:** People could create highly curated digital identities, spending much of their time in virtual worlds where they can

design an ideal self. This might strengthen self-centered views, as they become used to controlling every aspect of their image.
- **Artificial Intelligence Feedback Loops:** Personalized AI "assistants" might tailor content to the user's tastes. While convenient, such an echo chamber can reinforce self-obsessed beliefs. If the user only sees content that flatters their worldview, empathy for others could fade.
- **Wearable Devices for Constant Self-Tracking:** Health or performance-tracking tools can be beneficial, but if used excessively, they might feed a constant need to measure and display personal milestones. Rather than caring about how one's health choices affect family or community, the focus might lie on personal metrics.

Though technology can also spread messages of empathy and community, it may serve as a powerful mirror for self-focused habits if designers prioritize engagement and profit over genuine social connection.

Political and Civic Impact

If narcissistic traits become more accepted, politics could shift in ways that affect entire nations. Examples include:

1. **Public Figures Who Rely on Image Over Policy:** Voters might be drawn to leaders with grand, self-promoting styles, even if their actual plans are vague. This can lead to governance based on spectacle, with less attention to real issues like healthcare, education, or infrastructure.
2. **Partisan Polarization:** Self-obsessed leaders might feed division, framing all issues as a battle in which they must triumph. Their goal could be personal glory rather than unifying people. Over time, this might weaken institutions designed to serve the entire population.
3. **Less Public Trust:** If citizens regularly see leaders exaggerating personal achievements or deflecting blame, faith in government could deteriorate. Distrust of public officials might rise, making collaborative solutions to big problems (like climate challenges or economic reforms) harder to achieve.
4. **Grandiose Foreign Policies:** A self-obsessed leader might seek to dominate the global stage, dismissing diplomatic norms or alliances that require compromise. Such actions can create tensions between countries, complicating efforts to tackle shared global challenges.

On the other hand, a growing awareness of narcissism might also push voters to demand more humble, service-oriented leadership. If citizens recognize and reject performative politics, they may favor genuine problem-solvers, leading to more stable governance.

Cultural Shifts in Media and Entertainment

Art, television, film, and online content often reflect and shape social attitudes. If narcissistic outlooks remain on the rise, media might change in several ways:

1. **Reality Shows and Influencer Culture Expand:** Programs focusing on dramatic personalities might continue multiplying. Producers may cast those who are brash or self-centered because it attracts viewers. As a result, audiences become more familiar with self-obsessed behaviors, gradually seeing them as normal.
2. **Less Nuanced Storytelling:** Subtle, character-driven narratives might be overshadowed by stories centered on extreme vanity or rivalry. While some watchers enjoy these plots, a steady diet of such content can normalize interpersonal conflict.
3. **Hero Worship of "Confident" Figures:** Viewers might celebrate individuals who seem unwaveringly sure of themselves, even if that confidence lacks substance. Meanwhile, characters who show vulnerability or collaboration may be regarded as "weak."
4. **Shift in Role Models for Young People:** Adolescents could look up to celebrities and online personalities who show strong self-promotion. If kindness and humility do not receive as much coverage, it may skew the values children absorb from pop culture.

Yet, cultural counter-movements can emerge. Some creators may produce content emphasizing empathy, cooperation, and authentic relationships. Documentaries, web series, or films that highlight mutual support could draw an audience tired of vanity-driven programming. Over time, these efforts might balance out or even challenge self-centered trends.

Mental Health Trends

If narcissism spreads and becomes an accepted norm, mental health services may see shifts in the problems people bring in. Some possibilities include:

1. **Higher Rates of Anxiety and Depression:** Constant comparison, pressure to appear perfect, and fragile self-esteem can wear people down. Those who cannot keep up with the showy standard might feel inadequate, isolated, or depressed.
2. **Burnout from Endless Self-Promotion:** Trying to maintain a carefully curated image drains energy. People might struggle to relax, feeling they always need to be "on." This constant stress can lead to mood swings or exhaustion.
3. **Strained Family Bonds:** Therapists might notice increased family conflicts if older relatives or partners see younger generations as selfish, while younger ones view older folks as out-of-touch. This clash could echo in counseling sessions.
4. **Youth Struggling with Empathy:** Counselors in schools might observe more bullying or relational aggression if empathy grows scarce. Children might not develop the emotional skills to handle disagreements without hurting each other.

In response, mental health professionals could introduce fresh training programs or workshops on empathy-building, conflict resolution, and healthy self-esteem. Some might partner with schools, workplaces, or community groups to address self-obsessed behavior at its roots.

Collective Responses and Initiatives

Awareness of narcissism's rise may inspire certain steps from diverse sectors:

1. **Community Programs:** Neighborhoods might host events or discussions that emphasize cooperation, such as group cleanups or skill-sharing classes. These experiences can help foster mutual respect and reduce isolation.
2. **Education Reform:** Schools could add modules on emotional intelligence, ethics, and social responsibility. By helping students see that real growth

involves balancing personal goals with a regard for others, educators can counter excessive self-focus.
3. **Company Policies and Leadership Training:** Businesses might require leadership workshops that stress listening skills, team success, and fairness. They could reward managers who show empathy toward employees, modeling a different approach.
4. **Media Literacy Campaigns:** Groups can teach viewers to recognize manipulative or vanity-driven content. Encouraging a critical eye—asking questions like "What values does this show promote?"—can help shift tastes over time.
5. **Support for Innovations That Foster Connection:** Technology companies might develop platforms designed to spark real conversation rather than competition for attention. Examples include group-based problem-solving apps or moderated online communities with strict anti-harassment rules.

While not every campaign will succeed, the combined effect of many small efforts can shape culture. If enough individuals, families, and institutions push for respectful discourse and empathy, it can create a buffer against the spread of harmful self-obsession.

Balancing Individual Confidence with Collective Needs

It is important to highlight that valuing oneself or building confidence is not bad. Self-esteem can be a powerful engine for personal growth. The issue arises when these traits overshadow consideration for others. A world where people find self-worth and also show empathy could flourish. The challenge lies in guiding cultural practices so that confidence does not turn into arrogance or disregard for communal welfare.

In the future, we might see new models of leadership, communication, and personal branding that integrate humility. Leaders could showcase accomplishments while crediting their teams. Public figures might celebrate shared victories rather than only their own. Friends could take pride in personal achievements but still remain open to the happiness or suffering of those around them. If society moves toward that balance, narcissism could remain a trait limited to a small minority rather than a mainstream phenomenon.

Potential Silver Linings

Even if narcissistic behavior grows more common, there can be certain unintended benefits. For example:

- **Pushing Some to Reflect More Deeply:** Those who feel put off by the hype might turn inward, asking what they truly value. This could spur a renewed interest in genuine community-building efforts.
- **Encouraging New Creative Voices:** If mainstream media leans heavily into self-obsession, it might motivate indie creators to explore alternative themes like kindness, vulnerability, and empathy, providing fresh stories and role models.
- **Developing Stronger Self-Help Tools:** Therapists and life coaches may create new approaches specifically tailored to people battling narcissistic tendencies or those affected by them, improving overall mental health resources.

These silver linings do not justify harmful behavior, but they show how societies often respond to challenges by innovating in positive ways. Sometimes a cultural swing in one direction prompts a counter-swing that finds a healthier middle ground.

Ethical and Moral Considerations

As narcissism grows, ethical questions also come into focus:

1. **Responsibility of Influential Figures:** Should public personalities who command large followings—politicians, business leaders, celebrities—hold themselves to a higher standard of empathy and accountability?
2. **Role of Platform Owners:** Social media and tech leaders might face pressure to discourage harmful self-promotion or to design algorithms that reduce echo chambers. Balancing free expression with societal well-being can be complex.
3. **Duty of Educators and Parents:** How can families and schools teach children to pursue personal achievements without dismissing others' rights or contributions?

4. **Individual Moral Compass:** Each person might need to weigh the pleasure of external approval against the deeper satisfaction of nurturing honest connections. Do they chase every attention-grabbing opportunity, or do they step aside to support others' growth?

These considerations highlight that narcissism is not just a matter of personal preference. It touches on bigger questions about how we form societies and keep them fair, collaborative, and compassionate.

Preparing for a Future with Greater Self-Focus

If current trends toward self-promotion continue, communities may need proactive strategies:

- **Research and Data:** Sociologists, psychologists, and economists could study narcissism's effects at a societal level, informing policy decisions or corporate best practices.
- **Workplace Reforms:** Organizations might embed empathy training in employee onboarding, encourage cross-department mentorship, and evaluate leaders partly on interpersonal skills, not just profits or image.
- **Media Responsibility:** TV networks, streaming services, and online platforms might give more visibility to content that shows characters working together, resolving conflict civilly, and valuing each other's strengths.
- **Local Initiatives:** Town halls or local clubs can host talks on empathy, problem-solving, and respectful communication. This helps neighbors see each other as partners rather than competitors.
- **Personal Growth Pathways:** People can stay informed about narcissistic habits and remain open to feedback, choosing to refine how they present themselves online and in person.

Such measures do not eradicate all forms of narcissism, but they can moderate its spread, encouraging more balanced personalities and societies. Over time, the small daily acts of courtesy, listening, and genuine collaboration build a framework that counters self-centered extremes.

Conclusion

The future impacts of narcissism touch nearly every sphere: relationships, work, governance, culture, and even technology. If left unchecked, growing self-obsession could fuel distrust, fragment communities, and drain workplaces of valuable collaboration. Younger generations might struggle to develop emotional depth, while entire industries operate on flash rather than substance.

Yet, societies have ways to push back. Through education, thoughtful leadership, supportive technology, and a collective desire for authentic ties, we can shape a world that values self-esteem but also empathizes with the needs of others. Recognizing narcissism's potential to expand is the first step in choosing how we respond. Armed with awareness, each individual—from parents to policymakers—can make decisions that encourage a healthier balance.

In our final chapter, we will step back to reflect on self-obsessed behavior in a broader sense. We will revisit key insights from this book, addressing how knowledge of narcissism can guide us to build better relationships, encourage mutual respect, and foster growth in areas that matter most. This overall perspective reminds us why understanding narcissism is so critical: it is not just about labeling a trait—it is about living together in constructive, supportive ways.

CHAPTER 20: REFLECTING ON SELF-OBSESSED BEHAVIOR

We have traveled a long road through the many layers of narcissism—its early roots, its manifestations in childhood, adolescence, and adulthood, and the toll it can take on health, relationships, and society. In this final chapter, we will bring together the core ideas. Our goal is to revisit the main lessons learned, see how they connect, and show how understanding narcissism can empower us to protect our well-being and support healthier communities.

The Core Characteristics of Narcissism

Throughout this book, we identified several traits that define narcissistic behavior:

1. **Excessive Self-Focus:** A constant preoccupation with one's own image, achievements, or desires, often at the expense of other people's experiences.
2. **Inflated Sense of Importance:** Feeling that one's ideas, needs, or rules outweigh everyone else's. This includes a strong entitlement to admiration or special treatment.
3. **Low Empathy:** Difficulty recognizing or caring about others' feelings, leading to dismissive or manipulative tactics.
4. **Need for Approval:** While they seem confident, many narcissistic individuals depend heavily on external praise to feel secure. Criticism or lack of attention can trigger extreme reactions.
5. **Fragile Self-Worth:** Beneath the bravado lies fear of being exposed as less than perfect, which often drives the need to stay in control of how others view them.

These traits can surface in varying degrees. Some people show mild versions of self-obsession without causing real harm. Others exhibit more extreme patterns that lead to emotional abuse or dangerous power plays.

The Many Faces of Narcissism

We also saw that narcissism does not always wear a single mask:

- **Openly Grandiose Style:** Loud bragging, craving for spotlights, and flaunting of status.
- **Vulnerable Style:** Shy or anxious on the surface, but still expecting special treatment and reacting harshly when ignored.
- **Situational Narcissism:** Temporary bursts of self-obsession that appear under certain conditions, like sudden fame or power.
- **Persistent Personality Trait:** Long-term patterns across multiple life areas, from family life to career decisions.

Recognizing this variety helps us avoid the stereotype that narcissism always looks like loud arrogance. Sometimes it appears as subtle demands for attention, or small manipulations that keep the focus on one person's needs.

Early Signs and Lifelong Effects

Childhood and adolescence can reveal early markers—tantrums when not praised, controlling behavior in peer groups, or a refusal to follow rules. If unaddressed, these traits may continue into adulthood, shaping how a person forms friendships, romances, or professional ties. Over the years, we discussed:

- **Family Environment:** Narcissistic parents can pass patterns on to children, modeling entitlement or constant demands for recognition. Meanwhile, siblings might learn that the loudest or neediest child gets the most attention.
- **School and Social Influence:** Classmates, coaches, and teachers might reinforce self-obsession if they only reward showy talents. Teenagers' social media use can fuel the desire for likes, shares, and validation.
- **Adult Challenges:** Strong self-focus can undermine relationships. Friends may drift away, coworkers can lose trust, and partners may feel dismissed or controlled. Over time, the narcissistic individual may find themselves isolated or repeatedly in conflict.

These progressions reinforce the idea that narcissism is not just a personality quirk; it can shape an entire life path if left unchecked.

Harmful Consequences and the Importance of Boundaries

We devoted significant attention to the damage narcissistic behavior can do—both to the person showing it and to those around them. Constant arguments, manipulation, or blame-shifting can lead to:

- **Emotional Abuse:** Gaslighting, verbal attacks, or controlling tactics that erode a partner's or family member's self-esteem.
- **Physical Health Issues:** Chronic stress, anxiety, or depression among all involved. Strained relationships can trigger insomnia or digestive problems.
- **Workplace Toxicity:** Colleagues might leave, productivity can fall, and trust erodes if a self-obsessed manager or coworker dominates the environment.
- **Wider Social Problems:** At the societal level, a culture that glorifies self-promotion over substance can fuel division, shallow achievements, and short-sighted leadership.

Boundaries emerged as a strong antidote. Clear limits—along with direct communication—can protect others from being drained or controlled. They also send a signal that certain behaviors have consequences. Whether in friendships, families, or workplaces, boundaries help preserve dignity and create a fair space where everyone's voice can be heard.

Paths to Change

For individuals displaying narcissistic traits, genuine transformation is tough but not impossible. We explored various methods that can help:

1. **Therapy and Counseling:** Cognitive-behavioral approaches, group therapy, or family sessions can promote self-awareness. Though many narcissistic people resist opening up, the structure of therapy can gently guide them to see how their actions affect others.
2. **Empathy-Building Exercises:** Active listening, mindful reflection, volunteering, or perspective-taking activities can expand one's ability to care about others' viewpoints.

3. **Communication Training:** Learning to manage conflict, accept feedback calmly, and share credit can reduce tension in daily interactions.
4. **Self-Reflection Tools:** Journaling or mindful breaks can break the habit of constant self-promotion, leading to deeper understanding of one's motivations.

Not everyone with narcissistic traits will commit to these paths. Some only attempt them when threatened with losing relationships or facing career setbacks. But if they do engage sincerely, they might develop healthier self-esteem that does not rely on belittling others.

Handling a Narcissistic Individual

Meanwhile, for friends, family, or coworkers, we looked at day-to-day coping strategies:

- **Calm, Clear Communication:** Minimizing emotional flare-ups, keeping points short and direct.
- **Evidence and Documentation:** Using written records to settle disputes in professional settings.
- **Emotional Boundaries:** Deciding what to share, when to leave or end a conversation, and how to stay grounded.
- **Support Networks:** Leaning on trusted peers, counselors, or family members to counter the gaslighting or blame that a narcissistic person may push.
- **Knowing When to Walk Away:** In extreme situations involving abuse or persistent toxicity, stepping back or ending contact could be the safest route.

These actions protect one's mental health while maintaining whatever relationship or interaction is necessary. While the narcissistic person might still behave in self-centered ways, clear boundaries and well-structured communication help prevent their behavior from derailing everyone else's peace of mind.

Broader Societal Outlook

The previous chapter (Chapter 19) showed how narcissism can affect workplaces, schools, governments, and popular culture. Key concerns included:

- **Increased Distrust and Fragmentation:** If too many people adopt self-promoting habits, empathy can wane, leaving social bonds weaker.
- **Risky Decision-Making in Leadership:** Self-obsessed leaders may focus on personal praise at the expense of long-term social or economic stability.
- **Cultural Normalization of Vanity:** As media highlights grand personalities, quiet, genuine contributions might be undervalued.

But society also has ways to push back, such as:

- **Education Reforms:** Teaching empathy, ethics, and group work from a young age.
- **Workplace Standards:** Encouraging leaders to cultivate trust and share credit.
- **Community Programs:** Fostering cooperation among neighbors and local groups, showing real-life benefits of mutual support.

If enough individuals and institutions promote these values, the worst of narcissistic trends might be contained or reversed.

Finding Healthy Self-Worth

A critical lesson repeated throughout is that having confidence does not automatically equal narcissism. Healthy self-worth involves:

- **Acknowledging Strengths and Weaknesses:** Seeing oneself as capable yet imperfect, open to advice, and willing to learn.
- **Respect for Others:** Celebrating one's own progress does not require overshadowing another person's success.
- **Handling Setbacks Maturely:** A confident person can face failure, take responsibility, and adapt rather than lashing out or deflecting blame.
- **Empathy as an Asset:** Recognizing that helping others or being kind does not reduce one's own achievements. Instead, it enriches relationships and community life.

When people anchor their self-esteem in genuine accomplishments, moral values, and cooperative ties, they feel less need for the endless applause craved by narcissistic personalities. This approach to self-respect fosters resilience and fosters more positive interactions.

Personal Reflection and Growth

It is valuable to ask ourselves:

- **Do I catch myself bragging or seeking approval too often?** Recognizing a habit of self-promotion can prompt a decision to share focus with others.
- **How do I react when criticized?** If strong defensiveness arises, it might indicate a fragile self-image. Accepting feedback calmly can be a step toward healthier confidence.
- **Am I open to others' emotions?** Checking whether we actively listen and care about friends, coworkers, or family can highlight if empathy skills need strengthening.
- **Where can I practice generosity?** Offering sincere help or praise reminds us that contributing to someone else's well-being does not reduce our own worth. It can, in fact, deepen connections and personal satisfaction.

Small, daily choices—like listening fully during a conversation or acknowledging a coworker's effort—gradually shape a mindset that values mutual respect.

Encouraging Change in Others

When someone close to us shows self-centered tendencies, we might wonder how to help. A few guidelines stand out:

1. **Model the Behavior You Wish to See:** Practice empathy, fair-mindedness, and honesty yourself. Show that genuine confidence does not require constant self-praise.
2. **Offer Encouragement for Positive Steps:** If they make an effort to share credit or listen better, note it. This positive feedback can motivate them to continue trying.

3. **Hold Steady Boundaries:** Consistent rules on what is acceptable show them you take your needs seriously. Over time, they might respect those rules more than constant lectures.
4. **Resist the Urge to "Save" Them:** Over-involvement or endless forgiveness can enable harmful behavior. Change must come from within the individual. Your role is supportive, not controlling.

Recognizing that not everyone will change, and that you are not solely responsible for their growth, guards against burnout. Meanwhile, offering tools or gentle advice (if they are open) can still plant seeds that might sprout later.

Embracing Empathy and Collective Well-Being

A large theme is that empathy is not just a personal virtue—it is a cornerstone of healthy communities. By caring about others' perspectives, we reduce conflicts, share resources more fairly, and maintain respectful ties. Narcissism undermines these processes by narrowing focus to one person's image or desires. Therefore, each act of empathy or cooperation counters the spread of self-obsession. Whether it is a smile at a stranger, a listening ear for a coworker, or a willingness to share the spotlight, small gestures accumulate into a culture that values togetherness.

Final Insights for Readers

1. **Stay Alert to Harmful Patterns:** Understanding narcissism helps us spot red flags—gaslighting, manipulation, endless bragging—before they consume our lives. Early recognition can spare us deeper pain.
2. **Protect Your Well-Being:** Setting boundaries and seeking support is not selfish; it is necessary when dealing with a self-obsessed person. Everyone deserves respect in relationships.
3. **Aim for Balanced Confidence:** Pride in one's abilities is healthy, but it should not overshadow empathy. True self-esteem thrives on both self-assurance and regard for others.
4. **Encourage Healthier Environments:** Whether in families, friend groups, or workplaces, promoting open dialogue, fairness, and empathy counters narcissism's negative effects.

5. **Keep Hope Alive:** While some individuals or social trends may seem overtaken by vanity, there are always pathways for positive change. People can learn and grow. Cultures can shift direction.

The Ongoing Relevance of Understanding Narcissism

Even as we conclude this book, the conversation on narcissism continues. Psychologists, sociologists, and everyday observers keep learning about how self-obsession evolves in our world. The digital age, global challenges, and new social structures bring questions about how narcissism may adapt. Staying informed allows us to respond effectively—individually and collectively.

This knowledge does more than label a problem. It gives us tools to protect ourselves, remain compassionate, and encourage constructive behavior. Each person who practices or teaches empathy, sets fair boundaries, and invests in healthier self-esteem contributes to a world that prizes real connection. By acknowledging the pitfalls of narcissism, we stand stronger in creating relationships and communities rooted in mutual respect.

Conclusion

From the earliest hints of self-centered thinking in childhood to the complex ways narcissism can shape our adult lives, we have seen that this behavior reaches far beyond simple vanity. It can warp families, disrupt workplaces, fracture friendships, and fuel harmful trends in wider society. Yet, we have also seen that self-obsession is not inevitable nor invincible. With awareness and consistent effort, individuals can reshape their habits. Communities can embrace empathy and cooperation, dampening the appeal of pure self-promotion.

We hope the chapters in this book have given you a clear, accessible look at narcissism's many facets, along with practical guidance for safeguarding your well-being and encouraging healthier ties. Whether you face a narcissistic boss, a self-focused relative, or are reflecting on your own tendencies, remember that understanding is the first step toward positive action.

As you move forward, keep in mind the central lesson: confidence and self-respect can thrive alongside humility and concern for others. By supporting practices that blend personal growth with social awareness, we can shape environments where everyone's value is recognized. In doing so, the noisier, superficial demands of narcissism will find it harder to take root. Instead, honest connection, fair collaboration, and respectful communication can flourish, uplifting both individuals and the shared world we inhabit.

www.ingramcontent.com/pod-product-compliance
Lightning Source LLC
LaVergne TN
LVHW012107070526
838202LV00056B/5659